Language Learning in Ministry

Language Learning in Ministry
Preparing for Cross-Cultural Language Acquisition

Jan Edwards Dormer

Available at missionbooks.org

Language Learning in Ministry: Preparing for Cross-Cultural Language Acquisition

© 2021 by Jan Edwards Dormer

All rights reserved.

No part of this book may be reproduced, stored in a retrieval system, or transmitted in any form or by any means—electronic, mechanical, photocopy, recording, or otherwise—without prior written permission of the publisher, except brief quotations used in connection with reviews in magazines or newspapers. For permission, email permissions@wclbooks.com. For corrections, email editor@wclbooks.com.

Scriptures taken from the Holy Bible, New International Version®, NIV®. Copyright © 1973, 1978, 1984, 2011 by Biblica, Inc.™ Used by permission of Zondervan. All rights reserved worldwide. www.zondervan.com The "NIV" and "New International Version" are trademarks registered in the United States Patent and Trademark Office by Biblica, Inc.™

Published by William Carey Publishing
10 W. Dry Creek Cir
Littleton, CO 80120 | www.missionbooks.org

William Carey Publishing is a ministry of Frontier Ventures
Pasadena, CA 91104 | www.frontierventures.org

Cover and interior design: Mike Riester
Copyeditor: Andy Sloan
Managing editor: Melissa Hicks

ISBNs: 978-1-64508-323-8 (paperback)
　　　　978-1-64508-325-2 (mobi)
　　　　978-1-64508-326-9 (epub)

Printed Worldwide

24 23 22 21 20　1 2 3 4 5 IN

Library of Congress data on file with publisher.

To my parents, Max and Dixie Edwards,
thank you for your missionary service.

Thank you for giving me an identity that I treasure—that of being an MK.

Thank you for your perseverance and humility in learning a new language and culture that endeared you to those you served.

Above all, thank you for keeping your eyes focused on what really matters: living lives through which others can see Christ.

CONTENTS

Introduction   ix

1. Misconceptions about Language Acquisition   1
This initial chapter will address commonly held misconceptions about language acquisition, such as the notion that children pick up languages effortlessly and that full immersion in the target language is best.

2. Principles of Language Acquisition   17
This chapter will outline several important concepts of second language acquisition. Some of these are the importance of comprehensible input, the value of lowering stress, the notion of respecting a silent period, and the need to use the new language for meaningful communication.

3. Formal Language Learning   35
This chapter will outline what a good language learning course or school looks like. What kind of curriculum is followed? What kinds of methodologies are used? How do teachers interact with students? What tasks are given for meaningful language use?

4. Informal Language Learning   49
This chapter addresses informal, learner-driven language acquisition in two types of situations: (1) language acquisition in settings in which formal language study is not available; (2) the ongoing work of the language learner, after formal studies, to continue to acquire the language.

5. Children's Language & Educational Needs   59
This chapter addresses the needs of MKs with regard to language and K-12 education. It helps parents understand the relationship between language and academic learning, and provides a set of questions which can help parents make the best decisions for their children.

6. Opportunities for Ministry amid Language Learning   83
This chapter addresses ways in which the language learning process itself can contribute to ministry in the host country. The goal in this chapter is to paint the language learning period in the life of a missionary in an opportunistic light, showing the many benefits—for self, family, and ministry—which can result.

7. **Applying New Understanding to Chart a Path for Success**   91
This final chapter ties together the concepts throughout the book, inviting readers to apply them in designing a plan for their own and their children's language acquisition. Additional attention is given to considering how personal and family well-being will be maintained during the language acquisition process.

References   103

Appendices
    Appendix A: Language Proficiency Scales   105
    Appendix B: English for Life Curriculum   112
    Appendix C: Second Language Acquisition Self-Assessment   129
    Appendix D: Language Teaching Methodologies   133
    Appendix E: Language Learning Resources to Create   143
    Appendix F: Language Learning Online Resources   147

Acknowledgments   148

INTRODUCTION

My Story ... and Others' Stories

After I had spoken at a conference on MK (missionary kid) language issues, a cross-cultural worker said to me, "I sure wish I had known all this ten years ago when I was trying to learn Hungarian." I wasn't surprised, since I hear similar comments every time I have an opportunity to talk to cross-cultural workers about second language acquisition. Such statements always fill me with sadness, because the pain, angst, self-doubt, and sense of failure so frequently expressed concerning language learning usually could have been greatly reduced. More pleasant and positive processes and results are possible—if language learning is approached more realistically and strategically.

I come to this field of missionary language learning from multiple perspectives. First, I grew up in Brazil as an MK. In chapter 5, I will share about my own childhood language learning experience at age ten. Being immersed in a Brazilian school at that age, without support from the school, was quite difficult. Thankfully, we now know much more about childhood language learning and language immersion than was known back then.

While I was struggling in the Brazilian school, my parents were in a typical "missionary language school." I was old enough to see the stress they were under. Since my dad kept failing Portuguese grammar tests, at one point he was told that he should go back to America because he would never learn the language. So when we moved to interior Brazil, everyone was surprised that my dad, rather than my academically excelling mom, could better communicate with the people.

Perhaps these early experiences with language learning contributed to my interest in the field of second language acquisition, because shortly after earning a bachelor's degree in elementary education at Asbury College, I went on to pursue a master's degree in TESOL (Teaching English to Speakers of Other Languages).

Marriage and two daughters came next, along with pastoring a church in Ontario. But it wasn't long before my husband, Rod, and I felt God calling us to missions. We packed up and moved to Indonesia. and that's where the stress of language learning hit me full force. I was now an adult trying to learn a language that everyone was telling me was "easy." Hearing this just increased my frustration, as I struggled to memorize impossibly long words.

Rod was dealing with language and cultural adjustment in his own way: reading a lot of novels to escape the stress—and possibly to escape my venting about our language classes! I had been trained in language teaching, and yet none of my teachers were using the methodologies that I knew would help me learn. I felt that I didn't have the authority to suggest changes, so I ended up quitting formal classes much earlier than I should have.

After four years in Indonesia, we switched gears and headed to a new ministry in Brazil. I breathed a sigh of relief at the thought of going to a country where I already knew the language, but I underestimated the helplessness I would feel watching my daughters and husband try to learn Portuguese. Being the only one in the family who spoke the local language brought its own set of stressors as I grew frustrated trying to find the right balance of using Portuguese in the home to help them learn and knowing when and how much to offer help and feedback.

Meanwhile, I had been growing as a TESOL professional. As I developed different types of programs for teaching English in Indonesia and Brazil, I increasingly wondered about the disconnect between what we know to be "best practices" in teaching English as a second or foreign language and how I had experienced language learning as a missionary. My increased interest in the field of second language acquisition led me to pursue a doctorate in curriculum, teaching and learning—focusing on language acquisition—at the University of Toronto.

On the ministry front, we faced several unexpected turns in the road. After five years in Brazil, our permanent visas were not granted; so we returned to Indonesia. "This time," I thought to myself, "I will really learn Indonesian." Alas, once again I was in classes that were painfully ineffective, and again I did not persevere. Instead, I spent time talking with our helper, and became fluent with foundational language—the only language I felt I really needed, since all my ministry work was in English.

One remaining language learning experience came about because of a one-year stint in Kenya. Early in that year we spent three weeks in Tanzania learning Swahili. Now three weeks is certainly not enough time to learn a language. But it was in this program that I experienced, as a student, effective adult language teaching for the first and only time. The teacher used modern methodologies focusing on communication, and to this day I retain some of the understanding I gained about Swahili. Because the Kenyans we were working with spoke excellent English, however, I had little opportunity to use the minimal Swahili I had learned.

In my current role in TESOL education as part of a graduate program, I have opportunities to travel to conferences and retreats to speak about language issues to people who are ministering cross-culturally. The laments I have heard, such as the one in the opening line of this introduction, prompted me to engage in a research project—collecting data on how missionaries felt about their language learning experiences. I gathered surveys from 140 individuals, and followed up with a few of them. Although some certainly had good experiences, many did not. Many *did* eventually learn the language to a highly functional level yet still bore scars from their initial language learning period, speaking of it as a "desert"—a time they would like to forget. Some still struggled with the language after ten or more years on the field. Others left the field after one term, convinced that they would never "get" the language—some having been told that they couldn't have a ministry without high language proficiency.

A Better Way

These stories, coupled with my own experiences, have caused me to think that we might be able to approach the language learning of cross-cultural workers in a better way. We can provide more effective opportunities for language acquisition and better equip missionaries-in-training with an understanding of how additional languages are acquired. We can have a more realistic understanding of the role of language in communication in general, and thus in ministry effectiveness. We can better prepare families for their children's language learning needs and realities. And, possibly most importantly, we can frame the language learning experience as an *opportunity* for ministry, not merely as a prerequisite for it.

The Audience

Because this book is written in English, from the experiences and perspectives of a native English speaker, I assume that mainly native English speakers will find it relevant and applicable. So I geared my writing, for the most part, to those for whom English is their native language and who will be learning a *second* (as opposed to third, fourth, or more) language for their cross-cultural ministry. Many may have learned a smattering of a foreign language in high school or college, but most will not have gained significant communicative competence in that language.

That said, today's cross-cultural ministry force is blessedly diverse, with nations that formerly received missionaries now sending missionaries out, and formerly sending countries now also receiving missionaries. As linguistic and cultural diversity has increased in missions, many more questions about language have emerged. What should the common language among a multilingual mission team be? Should it be English if the native English speakers are in the majority and the nonnative English speakers have learned some English in school? Should it be the local language because everyone, after all, is required to learn it? But if so, what about those new to the field who haven't learned it yet? And what about the scenario in which one spouse in a marriage is native to the country of ministry, and thus speaks the language effortlessly, while the other spouse must learn that language in order to minister? How does second language acquisition play out for such couples? Does each person try to learn the other's native language? Or do they both just focus on the language of ministry?

These and other similarly sticky multilingual issues are not addressed specifically in this book. Nevertheless, I hope the principles highlighted here do provide good foundational knowledge for addressing questions such as these. One exception is found in chapter 5: when discussing children's language acquisition, I do briefly speak to the situation of missionary families whose native language is not English. When such families place their children in English-medium ("international") schools, they are essentially navigating three languages: their home language, the local language of the country in which they are ministering, and the language of the school. This brings its own unique set of challenges.

Appendices

As I sent my book chapters out to some very helpful readers for feedback, I was often asked if I was going to include something that person saw as important in regard to the provision of resources for language learning. My list of appendices grew with each suggestion! I do encourage you to return to the back of the book frequently for suggestions and resources for making your language learning more effective. Many more resources could have been included, and online internet searches can provide helpful ideas, as well as new applications, programs, and websites.

Word Choices

Finally, I want to share some of the choices I made regarding word usage. First, I want to unpack the wording of the title. In the main title, *Language Learning in Ministry*, the "in" is intentional. We can minister as we are learning language, and our learning of language should continue throughout our ministry. In the second part of the title, *Preparing for Cross-Cultural Language Acquisition*, the preposition changes to "for." An ideal time to utilize this book is prior to leaving for the place of service, as it can help to set the stage for success in language acquisition.

Second, I opted not to avoid using the word *missionary*, even though some organizations no longer use the term. I use the term *cross-cultural worker* wherever it is appropriate, but in some places the more traditional understanding of "missionary" seems helpful.

Third, I used masculine and feminine pronouns in this text randomly, sometimes referring to "he" and sometimes to "she" when talking about language learners. My use of either pronoun is not meant to imply any characteristic regarding either gender.

Lastly, I tried to avoid an overuse of technical, academic terms and jargon. Those reading this as professionals in the field of linguistics or second language acquisition may sometimes wish I had provided more specific or technical terminology, cited more experts, or gone more in-depth in my discussion of theories and research. However, my goal is to build understanding about second language acquisition, not to prove theories or teach terminology. Thus I tried to use common language, while still presenting accurate ideas. I hope that those who are interested in learning more will find the resources they need in the reference list provided at the end of the text.

Reach Out!

I love to hear from my readers! Please feel to reach out to me with questions or comments. I have many additional resources for language learning. My email address is jan.dormer@gmail.com. I look forward to hearing from you!

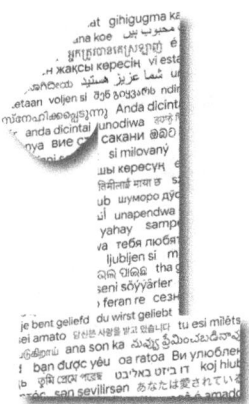

Misconceptions about Language Acquisition

PHIL *I really tried to learn the language for the first two years after we got here. But I just couldn't get it. I don't know why I thought I would. I've never been a good language learner. Now my kids, on the other hand—they're the lucky ones. Kids pick up languages easily, right? You should have heard our little Kaitlin when she was only four, jabbering away with the lady who came to clean our house. I wish it could be like that for me!*

Like Phil, many people have preconceived ideas about language learning, and these notions usually have some basis in reality. Phil may have taken Spanish in high school, yet not emerged from those classes speaking Spanish. And now Phil sees his four-year-old responding very differently to a new language environment than he is, and he quickly surmises that the difference has something to do with age. To complicate matters further, he assumes that he isn't a good language learner, because if he were, he would have learned Spanish in high school, right?

Upon closer inspection of Phil's beliefs, we see many unexamined assumptions. Among them are:
- that Phil's high school classes provided him with good language learning opportunities
- that some people can learn new languages and others can't

- that Phil could not have learned the same language that Kaitlin learned had he been exposed to the same interaction with the housekeeper
- that Kaitlin was using extensive and diverse language when she was "jabbering away"
- that Kaitlin did not experience stress from the new language environment like he did

Are these assumptions correct? What if they aren't, or what if they are just partial truths? Would that change Phil's perspective about language learning?

In this chapter we will examine commonly held beliefs and assumptions about language learning with the intent of determining if they are grounded in fact or if they stem from unexamined assumptions and experiences.

To begin, let's discover your current perspectives. Read the following statements, and then put an X somewhere on the line between "True" and "False" to indicate your level of agreement with the statement. Don't overthink your answers, but mark each line according to your initial reaction.

What Do You Think?

1. Children are better language learners than adults.
   True . . . . False
2. Children have fewer inhibitions than adults about using new language.
   True . . . . False
3. Children can hear and reproduce new sounds better than adults.
   True . . . . False
4. There is a "critical age" above which it is more difficult to learn a language.
   True . . . . False
5. Language aptitude tests are good at predicting language learning success.
   True . . . . False
6. Success in language learning is measured by the ability to communicate.
   True . . . . False
7. Some people can't learn new languages.
   True . . . . False
8. Language learning is quick and easy for some people.
   True . . . . False
9. The more you are immersed in a new language, the faster you will learn.
   True . . . . False

10. We learn a new language in a predictable sequence.
    True . . . . False
11. It's not important to understand how the language works; we just need to *use* it.
    True . . . . False
12. It usually takes no more than two years to learn a new language in an immersion setting.
    True . . . . False

Hang on to your answers! In the last chapter of the book we will revisit these statements to see what you have learned. Here, in this first chapter, I will address five commonly held misconceptions about language acquisition. I will present the basis for these beliefs and how a closer look at the complexity of language learning reveals that these statements can't simply be taken as fact.

Misconception #1:
Children Are Better Language Learners than Adults

I teach a graduate course on second language acquisition, and one of the first tasks I assign my students is to ask their family and friends this question: Who learns language more easily—children or adults? Inevitably the response comes back that *everyone* they asked believes that children learn languages more easily. Can something that nearly everyone believes actually be wrong? Yes! There is no shortage of examples of how something everyone believed was eventually proven false. For example, take the belief that the earth is flat, or that getting caught in the rain causes the flu.

As a society, we continue to build our knowledge, and commonly believed ideas continue to be challenged. To provide a more recent example, it wasn't long ago that coffee was seen as bad for you. Now, thankfully, through more research we know that coffee has some good properties as well. As a regular coffee drinker, I am grateful for that change in perspective!

"Second language acquisition," the term given to the learning of a new language after the native language has been acquired, is a relatively new field of study. Only in the past fifty years or so have we started to see scientific studies contributing to our understanding of how new languages are learned. We have learned a great deal about how the environment, the type of language being learned, and specific learning activities impact language acquisition. For example, we now have more understanding about how a child's interactions differ from those of an adult, and how this difference may explain why a child seemingly "picks up a language effortlessly."

Returning to our opening story, Phil's daughter Kaitlin likely heard simple and repeated phrases from the housekeeper every time they were together. Had Phil's housekeeper interacted with him in the same way, he might have been "jabbering" right along with Kaitlin!

Before we dive into some new understandings about child and adult language learners, let me define what I mean by a child language learner. Up to age three or four, one of a child's main tasks is the acquisition of his native language. When I refer to second language acquisition, I'm not talking about a child learning his native language. That is *first* language acquisition. And a child can have two first languages.

Children raised in bilingual homes truly do experience "effortless" language learning, in the sense that learning our native language(s) is unconscious and natural. (See more in chapter 5 about raising children bilingually—i.e., with two native languages.) In this chapter we are considering the scenario in which a child is learning a new language *after* the first language has been fully acquired. A four-year-old usually has good command of all the basic word sets (body parts, colors, frequent nouns and verbs, common adjectives, etc.) and the simple sentence structures of his native language. If he is exposed to a new language after this foundation in his native language has been acquired, we would call it a *second* language.

So what do we now know about the *second* language acquisition of children and adults? Let's consider the advantages that language learners might have at different ages.

Advantages of younger learners

For years, many have thought that there is a "critical period" in childhood beyond which language cannot be easily learned. This idea came from research on first language acquisition. It was theorized that a child who did not receive adequate linguistic input by a certain age (sometimes thought to be puberty) would not be able to acquire a native language. The idea of the "Critical Period Hypothesis" (CPH) was quickly adopted into common thinking about language acquisition. And unfortunately it has often been understood as applying to *second* language acquisition, even though this has not proven to be the case. In fact, Hakuta, Bialystok, and Wiley (2003) conducted a study designed to test if there is a decline in language acquisition after puberty, but found no such decline. They concluded that the CPH was *not* supported for second language acquisition.

There is one area of language, however, in which the notion of a "critical period" actually does apply: pronunciation. Children *do* appear to have superior ability to hear and reproduce new sounds. Some say that this ability also extends to the use of native-like speech in other areas as well, such as reductions (for example, shortening "going to" to "gonna"). The problem is that this advantage in pronunciation, or "native-like speech," is treated as more significant than it actually is. English, for example, has many dialects. What constitutes "native-like pronunciation"? And how important is that? An adult language learner might lament that she will probably never sound like a native speaker. But in the bigger picture of what constitutes communicating through a new language, it's just not that important.

Advantages of older learners

So ... Do adults have any advantages over children? Yes! In practically every other way, older learners—teens and adults—have the upper hand. Snow and Hoefnagel-Hohle (1982) conducted research with native English speakers of all ages who were learning Dutch as a second language. In their study, children three to five years old scored the lowest, in all categories, on language tests. Older children, teens, and adults all outperformed the youngest group of children.

One key area of superiority is in learning skill. Adults have been learning new things for many years. They have honed some learning strategies, understand the role of their own motivation and discipline, and have the ability to comprehend structure and organization. Children typically require far more repetition in order to remember a new language than do adults, because adults can consciously rehearse, practice, and memorize in a way that younger children normally cannot.

All this means that over the same period of time, given similar opportunity, adults are likely to learn far more words and language structures than a child.

Some cite emotional factors in claiming that children are superior in second language acquisition. For example, children are frequently said to have "fewer inhibitions." This does not jive with my experience of teaching children English in several different countries. Children are often shy and reluctant to use a new language. In fact, experts on English language learning in American schools affirm the "silent period"—a period of up to about six months during which a beginner in the language should not be required to speak. Contrast that with some very lively adult language classes in which students are willingly speaking out from the beginning, such is their investment in their learning.

The fact is, all personality types are found in all age groups. But older learners can consciously step out of their comfort zone to engage in an activity that will facilitate language acquisition.

Contexts for learning

All language acquisition is contingent on effective methods within an appropriate learning context. For example, an adult's superior learning ability won't be of much value if he has very little time and opportunity to use the language. And a child's natural ability in pronunciation can actually work against her if she is not exposed to proficient speakers.

Contextual differences are often at the root of the perception that children acquire languages more easily than adults. Imagine a child going to a new country and being placed in a local school. *If* the school has appropriate services for a child who is new to the language, this can be an ideal language acquisition context. (If not, it can be a very stressful and damaging experience. We will explore this more in chapter 5.) If the parents of this child are spending their days using their native language, and not engaged in learning the new language, then of course the child will outpace the parents in language acquisition.

However, the opposite can occur as well. Sometimes children are placed in international schools in the native language and have little contact with the new language. Their parents, on the other hand, may spend a rigorous year in language study. In this case the parents will learn the new language much more quickly and thoroughly, and the children may be at risk of not learning the language.

A final contextual reality is that childhood language use differs tremendously from that of adults. Childhood language is marked by very limited sentence types, a lot of repetition, and concrete rather than abstract language. The fact is that most adults could "pick up" this limited and concrete language in a very short time if they were permitted to interact like four-year-olds. This, more than any of the other issues, is likely what gives rise most often to the perception that children pick up language effortlessly. We fail to see that a child who is chattering away is actually using a very limited vocabulary and set of language structures. We also hear the native-like pronunciation of the child, and the hesitations of the adult, and leap to a false conclusion: the child has "picked up" the language easily, and the adult has not.

Misconception #2:
Some People Are "Good at Languages" and Others Are Not

A tale of two missionaries

I was ten when our family moved to Brazil. Our first year in the country was in a large city, where my parents were enrolled in language school to learn Portuguese. My mom loved academics and school. She had loved studying Latin in high school and had made excellent grades. So she thrived in the grammar classes, which characterized much of the language school experience. Her verb tense worksheets were perfect, and she consistently made A's.

Then there was my dad. He was not an academic; he thrived on interaction with people and getting things done. He had come from an active farm life and found it extremely hard to sit in a classroom facing a thoroughly uninspiring grammar book. Naturally, my father struggled. The verb conjugations baffled him. And whoever heard of gendered nouns? How could *shoes* be masculine and *pants* be feminine? It made absolutely no sense! And so he floundered in language school.

At one point, a well-meaning teacher came to him and said, "Mr. Edwards, you will never learn Portuguese. You should go back to your farm in America." But … there was no farm to go back to. My parents had sold everything to go to Brazil as missionaries.

After prayer, my dad returned to the teacher and said, "I know God brought us here. I will keep doing my best, and if he doesn't give me Portuguese, so be it. I am following God."

The year of language study came to an end. My mom passed with flying colors. My dad barely made it. But then we headed out to our place of ministry in interior Brazil, where my dad was going to develop a youth camp. My parents began interacting with the locals, and an interesting thing happened. My mom couldn't understand anyone, or be understood. You see, these people had never been to language school to learn "correct" Portuguese. The painstaking verb conjugations my mom had memorized? Not really a thing there!

You can imagine that my dad was in his element. He began making friends right and left. Everyone loved talking with him. His rudimentary Portuguese was a source of amusement, and my dad used this well. Our little church was packed when he preached because he elicited help from the audience. His sermons became very participatory, as people tried to help him find the right words.

My dad did not excel in grammar, but he did excel in communication. To this day, when I return to Brazil, people recount his language bloopers and speak of him fondly—even reverently. He had an impact on so many people. His impact was not diminished by his imperfect Portuguese, but quite likely was greater because of the humility he displayed through it.

People are differently gifted

I share this story to make the point that there are *many* different aspects of communication through a new language, and any given individual will have both strengths and challenges in these different aspects. My mom was clearly good at language from an academic perspective. She excelled at the book work. She understood the structures. She memorized well. But my dad was good at communicating. Unfortunately, we sometimes treat the language as an end in itself, rather than a vehicle for connecting with people.

And this is the main failure of traditional "language aptitude" tests. They measure one's facility with language structures and new sounds. But they don't measure a person's willingness to reach out and connect with a stranger through a new language. They don't measure one's flexibility in using gestures and facial expressions to make up for words that are unknown. And they don't measure one's heart and compassion for the people one has been called to serve.

I'm so glad my parents weren't given language aptitude tests to measure their fittedness for ministry in Brazil! I'm sure my father would have failed; and my life, and the lives of countless Brazilians, would have been much the poorer.

Misconception #3:
More Time Spent in the New Language Is Always Better

Our third myth is deceptive in that it is partially true. For sure, one can have too *little* language input. Take, as an example, foreign language learning programs in schools around the world. These classes often meet once or twice a week, for a total of one to three hours a week. This very limited time, often coupled with lackluster methods, can be so ineffective that it has been called an "inoculation against learning a language." For many people, high school foreign language classes not only did not result in speaking the language, but also fostered a distaste for language study.

But just because too little language input is ineffective, we should not jump to the conclusion that full immersion in the language is always best. Some interesting research alerting us to the fact that it is possible to have too much new language exposure comes from studies comparing English learners in both monolingual and bilingual schooling. If more exposure to the target language (the language one is learning) were always better, then we would expect English learners educated in schools that only use English as a medium of instruction to learn English more quickly. However, this is not what happens. Study after study (Collier and Thomas 2004; Cummins 1981; Ramirez, Yuen, and Ramey 1991) has shown that English learners who instead spend only *half* of their school day in English, and the other half in their native language, fare better. They make better progress in English and have the added advantage of also continuing to develop their native language. Why might a language learner make optimal progress with less than full immersion in the new language? Let's look at several possible reasons.

A saturation point
It seems there is a saturation point—a point beyond which you can have too much of a good thing. There are several factors that probably contribute to arriving at "saturation." First, there is fatigue. Plain and simple, language learning is exhausting. Most who have tried to learn another language can remember

times when struggling through a two-minute conversation felt like two hours. After just a couple of hours of language study, you wondered why you were so incredibly exhausted. After all, you hadn't really "done" anything! How could you be so tired?

The fact is, learning a new language, and struggling to communicate through a new language, leads very quickly to brain fatigue. And it's not just your brain. Your face can actually hurt from trying to make new sounds, and your body can ache from stress. Language learning fatigue is real!

Second, many language learning contexts are quite stressful. There may be the stress of having to communicate for meeting your and your families' needs, such as needing to be able to use the language to buy food or negotiate transport fare. Or there might be stressful classroom situations in which you are pushed to use language beyond your comfort zone, or during which you are compared with others and silently (or worse, not silently) shamed. Unfortunately, retreating from these stressors in some way (say, not going out to talk to the neighbors, or staying silent in class) for self-preservation brings on its own stress of guilt.

I will share more in chapter 2 about stress as an enemy of language acquisition, and the importance of lowering stress for optimal learning. But even in ideal language acquisition environments, fatigue and stress will be present and will produce a saturation point beyond which more engagement with the language becomes counterproductive. If a person is forced to engage with the language beyond this point, not only will language not be learned, but the lack of ability to escape from the language can have damaging effects. The language becomes the enemy. Motivation and self-esteem suffer.

And lest we think these effects are temporary and "worth the pain," I have spoken with missionaries who, years later, are angry and bitter about their early language learning days. Looking back on a language school experience that pushed students beyond their capacity, one individual said, "No one should have to go through what we went through. One person even tried to commit suicide." To reach a point of wanting to end it all is hopefully rare, but varying levels of depression while attempting to learn a new language is not.

Maintaining self and family

Even if fatigue and stress aren't overwhelming and the language learning load seems manageable, breaks are essential. Language learning frequently strips away our sense of self until we are able to find another version of ourselves through the new language. Thus, it is imperative to take some downtime to restore our sense of self. Most of us recognize the value of "self-care," and never is intentionality in this area more needed than when we are immersed in learning a new language.

For many people, maintaining their sense of self means having opportunities to be productively engaged in ministry or work through their native language. For some, it also means being able to retreat to their native language for simple pleasures like reading a book or writing emails to family. Unfortunately, many people feel that they should minimize these activities as much as possible, and instead use more of their time to study the language. Also, engaging in activities in the native language can produce guilt, which then counteracts their potential de-stressing effect. In reality, a person engaged in language learning should have the freedom to clock out at some point, saying, "I'm done for the day. I put in my X number of hours and did my X number of tasks. Now, for the rest of the day, I will focus on other things."

This perspective becomes especially important when there is a family to consider. I remember when my husband and I moved to Brazil with our two daughters, then eight and nine years old. Having grown up in Brazil, I spoke Portuguese. Countless people told me I should use Portuguese at home, with my family, to help them learn. I assumed they must be right, so we tried making the rule that dinner conversation would be in Portuguese. Guess what? Our previously lively dinner conversation ended. We no longer heard about our girls' days in school or what was bothering them. They didn't have the ability to talk about these things in Portuguese, so there was simply no dialogue. We decided that learning Portuguese wasn't worth sacrificing our home life. Home should be safe and accepting. Home should be where you can be honest and where you can be yourself. And home is rarely those things if family members are struggling to use a new language. (In chapter 5 I will share about the importance of children learning languages and address appropriate ways for that to occur.)

The good news is that it is usually sufficient if adults engage in effective language learning experiences for about 75 percent of a typical work week. The remainder of the time we can de-stress, re-engage in our native language, and take care of ourselves and our families by using our native language. Language learning won't suffer, and the time we do spend in language learning will probably be more profitable.

Misconception #4:
Language Learning Is Quick and Easy for Some and Painfully Long and Frustrating for Others

While there's no doubt that learning a language *is* painfully long and frustrating for some, we need to debunk the idea that those lucky few who inherited some kind of language learning gene can pick up languages easily, while others are doomed to frustration. Although individuals do experience language learning differently, there is no such thing as "quick and easy" language learning (except for true savants in languages), and those who are greatly frustrated with the process are probably experiencing a poor program. We can't pin all that frustration and ineffectiveness just on a person's lack of aptitude for languages.

What is actually happening when a person seems to learn a language effortlessly? As in the case of children, which we considered in Misconception #1, that perception often comes because a person can use a limited set of words and structures fluently. Some people do have a knack for picking up pronunciation (which isn't as big of a deal as some have made it out to be—rarely is perfect pronunciation needed in order to communicate). And if they also interact easily with people and aren't shy about using their new language, they can seem to have "picked up" much more than they really have.

This was my situation in Indonesia. Within a few months I had mastered the limited words and phrases that I needed in order to buy food and communicate with my house helper. And my pronunciation was good, probably because it was my third language. Indonesians would exclaim, *Lancar sekali!*—"Very fluent!" I fooled a lot of people with my fluency on very limited topics. Many Indonesians never knew that I didn't understand what they were saying as the conversation progressed beyond basic themes, because I was very good at nodding, smiling, and feigning comprehension. But that quick and early fluency made it hard for me to ask for repetition when I didn't understand; and as the years went by, that became harder and harder. I felt embarrassed to admit that I knew far less than people thought I did. So, quick but limited fluency can have a downside.

Another common scenario is when a person just loves languages and spends *a lot* of time working on a new language. Perhaps she has only been in the new country for a couple of months and is already conversing "fluently" with the neighbors. What we don't know is how many hours have been invested in language study during those two months. People who love learning a new language *do* spend many more hours immersed in the language than the rest of us. And because they enjoy the process, they pore over their language books, eagerly listen to recordings, and happily go out to talk with the locals to practice their new language. But if we count all the hours spent, it's still not *quick*. It still takes many hours. These people are just the lucky ones who love to spend their hours in this way. That's not most of us!

Do you identify more with those who find learning a new language a "painfully long and frustrating" process? So do I. I am not a language teacher because I love languages. I am a language teacher because it is a wonderful way to connect with people and serve them by helping them reach their goals. I enjoy seeing those who thought they could never learn English become successful as they experience effective methodologies in the classroom. When I have been in the language learner role, frustration and pain have been all too present.

People like you and me can benefit from considering the following research:

- Everyone can learn a new language. Language acquisition is not linked to intelligence or special abilities, although individuals have different areas of strengths and weaknesses, just as they do in the use of their native language.

- Language acquisition requires a lot of time for everyone. Some experts have suggested that two thousand hours must be invested in focused and effective language study and use in order to reach a high-intermediate or advanced level. In terms of years, Collier (1989) found that five to seven years are required for an adult to reach a competency level that includes being able to engage in academic tasks such as taking a college course. And this number of hours or years may be even higher depending on the "language distance" between your first language and the language you are learning. For example, it takes more time for a native English speaker to learn Chinese than German, because German is much more similar to English than is Chinese.

- Most people simply have to put in the time, which is why it makes sense to include language acquisition as a significant part of a missionary's job during his or her first term. Formal language study may only last a year, but the subsequent years are crucial for applying that learning and furthering language skill.

- Most people can acquire a language well without undue frustration. Given an excellent program of study and ideal learning conditions, acquiring a new language will likely be hard and take perseverance, but frustration beyond what is normal in day-to-day cross-cultural life is not a requirement. That said, ideal language learning conditions frequently are not present, and there often is significant frustration. This reality, though, should cause us to look for ways to change conditions instead of believing those feelings are just part and parcel of learning a language.

Misconception #5:
There Is a "Right" or "Best" Way to Go about Learning a Language

For much of the 70s and 80s, second language acquisition theorists and researchers were engaged in a search for the ideal method—a language acquisition magic bullet. If only the perfect method could be found, language acquisition could proceed methodically and predictably. That era ushered in some very interesting language learning methodologies. In one, "Community Language Learning," students were cast as participants in a support group. In another, "The Silent

Way," the teacher was largely silent, directing students to complex phonetic charts to figure out the sounds of the language. Time ultimately proved that there is no one single magical method that can guarantee language learning success for everyone. That said, each new method helped further our understanding of the complexities of language acquisition.

There *are* some absolute requirements for language acquisition. For example, one must have input, or exposure to the language—that is, one must hear or read the target language. And this input must be comprehensible. You must have some way of knowing what the sounds or words mean. Also, you must spend time using the language—reading, writing, speaking, and listening. If you are learning a language, you will be doing at least one of those activities.

Chapter 2 is dedicated to addressing these and other concrete, current understandings of how people—*all* people—learn languages. But first let's consider the limitations of those commonalities, looking at some ways in which language learners differ.

Language learner traits and variance

Here are three traits that have been identified as helpful in language learning but in which learners often vary significantly:

- *Tolerance of ambiguity.* This trait pertains to the ability not to fixate on the unknown language but to attempt to get the gist of something the learner reads or hears. While tolerance of ambiguity is considered to be a helpful trait in language learning, individuals will differ in their level of comfort with ambiguity. Some people are more "tolerant" than others. While people might be able to consciously improve in this area, if they aren't naturally comfortable with ambiguity it may not be worth the stress of trying to become more tolerant. Those individuals might be better off finding other language learning strengths and focusing on them.

- *Willingness to communicate.* This trait is characterized by a person's effort to engage in communication even when lacking some of the necessary words and structures. Some individuals aren't bothered if they lack the right words; they still want to communicate. Others experience extreme stress if they don't have all the right words and phrases in order to communicate. Although second language acquisition theorists have assumed that those with a high "willingness to communicate" are better language learners, more recent research has shown that individuals who do a lot more listening than speaking can also be successful—especially if that is the expectation within a certain cultural context.

- *Search for patterns.* Second language acquisition theorists have long believed that being able to see the patterns and structure in language is helpful in language learning. In fact, this belief is the premise for portions of most language-aptitude tests. This ability certainly figures prominently in understanding the grammar of a new language and being able to manipulate grammatical features. It has limitations in predicting communicative success, however, because individuals can usually communicate without perfect grammar or with grammatical phrases learned as language chunks rather than grammatical features.

Language learner preferences, interests, and personalities
Other obvious ways in which individuals vary is in their personalities, preferences, and interests. Although it should be commonsense that we will learn best when we are engaged in tasks or topics that interest us, some language classrooms, and even some approaches to self-study, seem to miss this point. Since I enjoy cooking, I am much more likely to engage in effective language acquisition through a cooking (and eating!) class than I am by struggling through a newspaper article about the founding of a city. But for my history-buff husband, such an article, followed by a trip to the city's museum, might be very effective.

Learners also vary tremendously in their learning preferences. While research doesn't support the existence of different "learning styles" per se, learners undoubtedly have *preferences* in learning activities, classroom environments, teaching styles, and more. Some love figuring out the grammar and doing traditional grammar/translation work. Others prefer just to sit down with a willing listener and struggle through a conversation. When it comes to learning new words, which is a huge piece of initial language learning, some enjoy traditional flash-card memory work, while others will invest more in learning if they can use an interactive app on their phones.

Learners obviously have different personalities as well. Some are more outgoing and others more introverted. Some are more task-oriented and others more event-oriented. Some are more attentive to details and others focus on the big picture. While none of these differences characterize either poor or effective language acquisition, they can dictate the types of activities through which we might best achieve success and maintain motivation for language acquisition.

In chapter 2 we will note some cautions regarding a "Do what interests you" approach. It is possible to engage in just one thing that you enjoy, such as doing grammar worksheets, and not see the expected result of being able to hold a conversation. While language work can be personalized, it also needs to be strategic. The important point here is that "Do what you like" has truth to it. The more that language learning activities can be fun and interesting for you, the more successful you will be.

Language learner needs
A final significant way in which learners differ is the very reasons why they are studying the language. Will they need to preach and teach at a graduate level in the new language? That is a very different goal than for those whose ministry will be through their native language and who therefore just need the local language for social purposes. These two groups may be able to start out with the same language learning program, but very quickly their paths will diverge.

Language learners may need to achieve different levels of ability in reading, writing, speaking, and listening. And within these four domains, they may need different language genres or registers. Two individuals may both need to develop writing skills, but one may just need to know how to write emails and informal notes, while the other needs to be able to fill out complex government forms. Where speaking is concerned, one person may need accurate, "correct" speech, while another may be better served in ministry by learning to speak the way local people speak, even if it isn't "correct." Such was the case of my dad!

Because of these ways in which language learners and their language needs vary, we should be wary of any approach or expert claiming a lockstep and foolproof pathway to language acquisition. Many such approaches have some good features that can help you learn, but if you aren't able to bring your own personality, preferences, and needs to your learning, you will likely experience some of the pain and frustration that we now know does *not* have to dominate the language learning experience.

Conclusion

I hope that our investigation into these five misconceptions has helped to bring you to a place of optimism about your own language learning. I trust that any damaging preconceptions have been diminished and that you will come to our next chapter with an open mind. Let's discover more about how people learn new languages!

Principles of Language Acquisition

HANNAH

Going to church is one of the most discouraging times of the week for me—and I hate it that I dread going to church! I never understand the sermon, even though I think I understand lots of words that I hear. But it's so frustrating that after a whole year here I still can't understand my pastor's sermons. The choruses are the only thing I actually enjoy. When they sing songs with simple and repetitive lyrics, it's great. I can actually worship sometimes! But ... what am I doing wrong? What do I have to do to start understanding higher-level language, like sermons?

Hannah's feelings are shared by many who struggle with going to a church that uses a new language. Why can't she understand sermons by now? Is there something she should be doing differently? In this chapter we will dive into the field of second language acquisition. We will look at both what is known and what is not known, and see where this field of study is headed.

What Is Second Language Acquisition?

Second language acquisition (SLA) is the study of how people learn additional languages after acquiring their native, or first, language. We saw in chapter 1 that a child has usually acquired her native language by around age four, and a new language introduced after that point would be considered a second language. Children learning two languages from birth actually develop *two* native languages. We will explore this more in chapter 5.

One important thing to understand about SLA is that this term is generally used even when the language being learned is a person's third, fourth, or seventeenth language. Though phrases such as "learning an additional language" are also used, the learning of any language subsequent to the native (first) language is still commonly referred to as SLA. Another term to clarify is *acquisition*. Though language *learning* and language *acquisition* are often used interchangeably, we will see that the word *acquisition* is the more precise term to indicate the process of developing full communicative competence. When a person is able to use a language to communicate with others, we can say the language has been acquired. *Learning*, on the other hand, sometimes refers to gaining knowledge about the language by studying its grammar and vocabulary.

A Short History of the Study of SLA

The field of SLA study began developing in earnest in the mid-1900s. Early theories of SLA were derived from studies of how children acquire their *first* language, with the assumption that acquiring additional languages must be similar to acquiring a first language. Over time, second language acquisition came to be seen as a separate, though similar, process. Theories about and methodologies for SLA flourished throughout the latter half of the 1900s. The new millennium has seen a focus on research studies carried out to confirm or disprove theories, and increased research involving brain studies have been made possible thanks to innovative technology.

We will look at four theoretical perspectives of SLA (Lightbown and Spada 2013). Each has sought to explain a piece of the SLA puzzle, and each has added some clarity to the complexity of how we acquire additional languages.

The behaviorist perspective

One of the earliest explanations of SLA came from the era of B. F. Skinner, who wrote *Verbal Behavior* in 1957 (Chomsky 1959), and his studies on behaviorism. Learning a new language was seen as a stimulus and response process: a person hears new words, repeats them, and thus learns a language. The most well-known approach to emerge from this perspective was "audiolingualism, or the "audiolingual method" (ALM). Developed initially for military uses, ALM spread internationally, resulting in the installation of language laboratories around the globe—places where students could put on headphones, put in a cassette tape, and *hear and repeat* over and over again. Through ALM, drilling, repetition, and memorized dialogues became synonymous with language learning.

Although ALM has taken a backseat to newer and more eclectic approaches, this era did bring to light an enduring concept in SLA: the characteristic of *automaticity*. ALM's drills and repetition caused students to learn phrases and dialogues to the point of being able to reproduce them without thinking. We now understand that a degree of automaticity is essential for language use. Oral communication is very fast. When some language components are available to us automatically, without conscious thought, our brains can devote thinking power to those aspects that do require thought. For example, if I ask, "Where did you go last weekend?" you don't have to devote much brain power to framing the words "I went …" Those two words come to mind automatically, leaving you ample cognitive space to think about where you actually went, in order to complete the sentence.

The innatist perspective

In the mid-twentieth century, Noam Chomsky's (1959) theories about first language acquisition were revolutionary in the budding field of linguistics. He proposed the concept of "universal grammar"—i.e., that languages share many similar structural features. He also argued that humans have within them a "language acquisition device"—i.e., a theoretical mechanism ensuring the acquisition of a native language. Chomsky brought in the perspective that children acquire their first language as an *innate* process, like walking and eating. Our brains and bodies are hard-wired for language acquisition, and thus it is nearly impossible for a normal developing human baby, even given vast diversity in the amount and type of exposure to language, *not* to acquire a language.

Later theorists applied Chomsky's ideas to SLA. Probably the most well-known second language theorist associated with the innatist perspective is Stephen Krashen (1981). His "monitor model" includes five hypotheses:

1. *The acquisition–learning hypothesis:* We *acquire* language through exposure, but we *learn* language through study.

2. *The monitor hypothesis*: The *acquired* system initiates utterances, but the *learned* system monitors and edits them.

3. *The natural order hypothesis:* Language features are acquired in a predictable sequence, which is roughly the same for all language learners.

4. *The input hypothesis*: Acquisition occurs when the learner is exposed to language that is comprehensible but a bit above the learner's current operational level. In other words, the learner needs to receive *comprehensible input*. Krashen illustrates this theory as "i+1," where *i* represents the learner's current level and +1 represents the step above that level.

5. *The affective filter hypothesis*: A person's general emotional state affects language acquisition, either facilitating or hindering it.

As a result of the work of Krashen and others, we saw, during the latter part of the twentieth century, a shift in language instruction from a focus on grammar rules and drills to a focus on communication. Still widely followed today, "communicative language teaching" (CLT) focuses on learning language through real communication, rather than through isolated vocabulary and grammar study and drills to perfect pronunciation.

The cognitivist perspective

Following on the heels of innatism came an increased focus on the cognition, or conscious mental processes, that are involved in SLA. Critics of innatism hypothesized that language acquisition can be explained in the same way that any other learning is explained. In other words, language wasn't "special," and general learning theories could account for SLA, just as they can account for, say, learning the times tables or learning to ride a bike.

Although most individuals reading this book will probably appreciate the innatist perspective, which for me means that God has designed us with a built-in capacity for language acquisition, the acquisition of *additional* languages probably can't be fully explained without the addition of active learning, or cognition. This perspective has added some key insights to our understanding of SLA. For example, Krashen theorized about the need for comprehensible *input*, through listening or reading. But while learning may begin with comprehensible input, it probably can't proceed very far without adding *output*, through speaking or writing. Swain (1985) coined the term "output hypothesis," arguing that it is only as students attempt to communicate with others that they become aware of areas in which they still need language development.

Another key insight from the cognitivist perspective is the importance of *noticing*, or *awareness*. For example, an English learner may not internalize the *-ed* word-ending to signal past tense until he begins to notice the *-ed* endings on verbs. Noticing alone does not result in acquisition, but it is the first step. This need to *notice* and *attend to* word forms, sounds, structures, and other features of language has resulted in the emergence of a strategy known as "focus on form."

In a classroom learning context, the teacher would briefly focus on the form of language, so that students can be more successful in the meaningful communication tasks that comprise the bulk of the class time. For example, while students are involved in the communicative task of writing an email telling what they did on the weekend, the teacher might ask them to pause for a few minutes to listen to a quick explanation of past verb forms and check all their verbs for that tense. This focus on structure at the very time at which it is needed for a particular communicative task is the ideal way to bring the cognition, or learning, piece into the broader experience of language acquisition.

The sociocultural perspective

The last perspective we will discuss focuses more on the social conditions for learning than on what happens in the brain. Vygotsky (1978) hypothesized that there is a "Zone of Proximal Development" (ZPD)—a zone in which a person can make progress toward a learning goal if assisted by someone who is a little further along in that development. Vgotsky's ZPD describes development in general, not language development specifically. However, it has been thought to aptly illustrate the reality that language learners can progress in the language as they interact with those who are more proficient.

You may recall Krashen's "i+1" theory and see similarities to Vygotsky's ZPD. Both can be understood well through the analogy of climbing a ladder. Krashen's i+1 emphasizes the importance of the *input* being at the right level for the language learner. In other words, the next rung on the ladder needs to be linguistically accessible—easy enough to reach. ZPD, on the other hand, highlights the notion that *interaction* must be available at that level. In other words, someone further ahead on the ladder is reaching down to help you up to the next rung.

Brain Research

The exciting new cutting edge in language acquisition studies is brain research. In the area of first language acquisition, researchers have gathered data about how babies process language. We now know, for example, that out of the roughly six hundred consonants and two hundred vowels found in human languages, babies begin to show preferences for the forty or so present in their native language well before their first birthday, and baby babbling shows signs of differentiation according to what language is heard by ten months of age (Kuhl 2010). This may explain the reality that young children do have an advantage in the area of pronunciation.

Another fascinating discovery in brain-related language research is the necessity of social interaction. In one study, infants displayed a much greater awareness of sound differences in a foreign language introduced at nine months when the language was spoken by a loving caregiver, as opposed to being provided through video (Kuhl 2010). And even if infants are exposed to a multitude of nonlanguage sounds, the language sounds coming from a human in close proximity is what they will attempt to imitate.

Francis Bailey and Ken Pransky (2013) produced a webinar entitled "Implications and Applications of the Latest Brain Research for English Language Learners and Teachers," which can be more broadly applied to the teaching and learning of all languages. According to Bailey and Pransky, brain research is confirming many SLA theories:

- Language *use* results in language acquisition—not discrete item learning. Students have to speak to develop speaking, write to develop writing, etc.
- Emotional factors override intellectual input.
- Working memory, which is our most fragile memory system, is limited in time and capacity to about seven new items in one period—such as a typical class period.
- Long-term vocabulary learning only happens by using new words in context.
- Our working memory in our second language is smaller than in our first and is most efficient when working with patterns. This is why it is so important to learn new words and structures in context.
- We can process a lot more information if we can "chunk" it. Some "chunks" of language should be rote learned to the point of automaticity. For example, it is helpful for English learners to learn "at night" and "in the morning" as memorized language chunks, rather than trying to remember rules for using the correct prepositions—*in* and *at*.
- Attention is important in language acquisition. We don't learn passively, but actively. Attention span can be calculated as age plus or minus two minutes. For example, a ten-year-old has an attention span of eight to twelve minutes. It's important to know, however, that attention span maxes out at about twenty minutes for adults.
- Students often experience cognitive overload in language classes. Signs of overload include confusion, distraction, expressions of frustration, and failure to connect new information to old.
- Students can process more information if it is meaningful.

Brain research through the use of ever-evolving technologies is just beginning. We will continue to learn more and more about how people acquire languages, and that will enable us to continue honing our understanding of how to most effectively teach or learn a new language.

Insights from Language Teaching

As we continue to unpack what we know about second language acquisition, we can also turn to the field of language teaching. While SLA studies certainly feed into language teaching practice, language teaching itself has also been the source of theories and practices in language acquisition that have proven to be viable and effective.

We will look here at one particular framework for second language teaching, outlined in two widely used and very practical texts for teaching English as a

Second (ESL) or Foreign (EFL) Language: *Teaching ESL/EFL Listening and Speaking* (Nation and Newton 2020) and *Teaching ESL/EFL Reading and Writing* (Nation and Macalister 2020). The authors suggest there are four essential components in a language class or course, each comprising roughly a quarter of the total language instruction time:

- Input (through listening and reading)
- Output (through speaking and writing)
- Fluency development (in reading, writing, speaking, and listening)
- Language focus (conscious study of language, such as grammatical forms, vocabulary, and pronunciation)

In this model, only about one-fourth of language learning time, or *language focus*, should be spent in focused study of language, such as in grammar worksheets or memorizing lists of words. The bulk of the time needs to be spent *using* the language for meaningful communication. This use involves meaningful input—when we are hearing or reading something that we want to understand and that is within reach of our abilities so that we *can* understand it. This is often intertwined with output—when we respond through speaking or writing in order to communicate our ideas—again, at the level at which we are able to communicate. The remaining quarter of language learning time should be spent on *fluency development*. Whereas with *input* and *output* we are reaching a bit to understand and use new language (Krashen's i+1 theory), *fluency development* occurs when we are already familiar with all the language we are using. We need opportunities for meaningful repetition with language that we already know in order to reach a point of automaticity and become fluent.

It may bear mentioning here that failure to acquire a language by taking a traditional course in a foreign language may be explained by the fact that many such courses essentially flip Nation's model. Traditional language classes often consist of 75 percent language focus and only 25 percent meaningful language use. If you weren't successful in high school or college language classes and thus think of yourself as a poor language learner, you may need to reallocate the blame for that failure to the design of the course and curriculum. Most people need to spend the majority of their language learning time in various forms of meaningful communication in order to acquire a new language. If your teacher had you doing grammar worksheets most of the time … it wasn't your fault that you didn't end up speaking the language.

What about Culture?

Language and culture are inextricably intertwined. Aspects of culture are acquired along with nearly every piece of language, and communication skills are enhanced through focused attention to culture learning. The fact that I don't devote a great deal of space to culture in this book is not a statement about its importance. Rather, my experience has been that courses, books, and other resources on the topic of cross-cultural learning and adjustment are relatively abundant in comparison to resources for acquiring a new language. Still, a few words about culture as it connects to language can add to our understanding of SLA.

First, it is important to understand that learning a new language is not simply learning a new "code" for the same ideas. Word to word translation may be possible for some ideas, but for many it isn't that straightforward. For example, the English word *be* can be translated into Spanish as either *ser* or *estar*—two words that have very different meanings. Language is used in ways which enact the culture, and the culture also impacts the way people use language.

Second, the fact that culture is acquired alongside language underscores the emphasis throughout this chapter on *meaningful communication*. While it is possible to learn phrases and translate passages through class-based academic tasks, students often find that words and phrases are used differently, or interpreted differently, when they hear them in authentic contexts and attempt to use them for real, meaningful communication.

I had an experience shortly after arriving in Indonesia that can help illustrate these points about culture and language. We had enrolled our four-year-old daughter, Jenna, in an Indonesian preschool. Lacking a vehicle, we hired a horse-cart driver, a *dokar*, to come pick us up each morning and take us into town to the preschool.

One morning the driver didn't come, and I panicked. How would I get Jenna to her class? I went outside and asked my neighbor something resembling, "Do you know where the dokar is?" Her response was simple and to the point: *Tanggal merah*. I was pleased that I understood this! She had said, "Red date." OK then.... But what did that have to do with the driver not coming? This was the question that I couldn't verbalize in Indonesian.

Seeing that I was upset, my neighbors went to fetch the dokar. He soon pulled up in front of our house. But they all kept saying, "Tanggal merah! Tanggal merah!" I still didn't have a clue what "red date" meant in connection to my daughter's preschool. I insisted that the driver takes us to town. He humored me, and off we went. Upon arriving at the preschool, I discovered that no one was there. And the driver said, for the twentieth time, "Tanggal merah."

It was only then that the cultural meaning of "red date" dawned on me: It was a holiday! A "red date" was a day when schools and businesses were closed. How could I not have known that? Here's what threw me: I had learned the word for "holiday," and they weren't saying that word, so it never crossed my mind that this was a holiday. What I had not learned was the colloquial, informal way of referring to a holiday: tanggal merah.

Those who have tried to learn another language in another culture usually have similar stories to tell. Communication is about much more than learning words and structures. And that *more* is how those words and structures are bound up in daily activities, values, and social norms—in other words, culture.

Putting It All Together: What We Do and Don't Know about SLA

Where does this leave us? I will close this chapter with a list of eight key words or phrases—concepts impacting second language acquisition. For each, we will see what SLA experts know and what we still have yet to learn.

Input

One cannot learn a language without being exposed to it. But this exposure, or input, through listening and reading, must be *comprehensible*. We can't acquire language that we don't understand. Further, input should be meaningful, engaging, and embedded in a social context (or a simulation of such in a classroom). This allows us to acquire both language and culture as we navigate specific contexts. What makes language input comprehensible? The use of visuals, objects, facial expressions, and actions can help us comprehend. Some experts (e.g., Nation 2020) suggest that 5 percent is the ideal percentage of new language in a given situation. In other words, if we already understand 95 percent of a text, we are able to comprehend the remaining 5 percent. Likewise, if we already understand 95 percent of something we hear, we can reach to understand the new 5 percent from context.

While it is helpful to know that we acquire language incrementally through exposure to just a little more language than we can understand, in practicality, individuals who live among those who use the target language are typically exposed to lots of language they don't understand. Is this a problem? The answer probably depends as much on personality as on SLA theory. Recalling the story at the beginning of this chapter, it's clear that Hannah would be much less frustrated if she could hear a sermon at her language level. But sometimes that just isn't possible. Sometimes we work through difficult texts with more than 5 percent new language, and we do learn some language in the process. Sometimes we only understand a fraction of what is said as we participate in a conversation, but we do grow a little in our comprehension through that fraction. Sometimes we are exposed to much more language than that which is comprehensible, yet we do still learn language.

What is unclear is the impact this has on overall language acquisition over time. At what point does the stress of dealing with input that is not at the right level begin to impede language acquisition? When does it lessen motivation and hinder comprehension of even what might have otherwise been understood?

SLA experts also may not yet understand how the brain might be working to filter out what is not comprehensible, focusing instead on the part that a person can understand and learn from. In short, we know that comprehensible input is needed, but we still have a lot to learn about what it might look like across very diverse contexts and individuals.

Output

Though there are no doubt some individuals whose only need is to comprehend language through reading or listening, for the vast majority of language learners acquisition includes output—the ability to speak and maybe also to write in the new language. When a person is just beginning to learn a language, there can be a *silent period*—a period of time just to listen and read in the new language before being expected to produce it. As I mentioned earlier, some language teaching approaches are built around this premise, valuing *reception before production*. In many other situations, though, language learners are expected to speak and write in the new language very early on. Some learners do well with this "pushed output," while others would benefit from a more flexible approach, allowing them to begin speaking when they are ready.

Output plays a key role in second language acquisition, as it gives a learner an opportunity to find out how much he knows (Swain 1985). It is often only as we begin using a new language that our attention is drawn to word forms, grammatical structures, and other language features, providing opportunities to test, confirm, and modify our language. When we are trying to use the new language in speaking or writing, ideally we will be receiving "corrective feedback" from a teacher or other proficient speaker. Most language learners benefit from feedback which helps them correct errors and improve in accuracy.

Nation (2020) claims that output should comprise about 25 percent of our total language learning time. There is evidence, as well, that the lack of opportunity for output that we see in some K-12 contexts in which students are learning a new language through their schooling contributes to incomplete acquisition. There *must* be opportunities to speak language in order for children to acquire it fully. However, the case of adult language learners may not be as clear-cut.

Some research suggests that the amount of desired output may hinge on cultural and contextual factors, and that language can be acquired just as proficiently by those who are shy, for example, and reluctant to speak, or in contexts in which students aren't expected or allowed to speak much in class.

My own recent research on the language acquisition experiences of cross-cultural workers suggests that harm is done when adult learners are forced to speak before they are ready, especially outside of the classroom context. So it may be important to consider the fact that research is not all that clear about how much output is needed, and at what language levels, and to err on the side of letting learners determine when they are ready to speak and write.

Interaction

Language learning should be relational. It is clear that interaction—making a new friend, asking for directions to the subway, exchanging emails regarding families—is often a cornerstone of successful language acquisition. While computer programs, apps, and videos or TV can provide some language input, the input that comes through human interaction is different. Emerging brain studies even suggest that personal interaction may involve different parts of the brain, facilitating increased neurological connections.

Although it can be helpful to interact with those who know more language, interaction with other learners at the same level can be just as effective. Research tells us that learners who interact with each other don't produce more errors overall than those who just interact with proficient speakers, such as their teachers. In other words, hearing mistakes doesn't necessarily make you more likely to make those mistakes, as long as there is also sufficient opportunity to hear correct forms.

That said, the amount and type of interaction for optimal language acquisition has not yet been defined. For example, how do classroom simulations compare to real contexts? Are they more effective? Less effective? What truly makes interaction meaningful and engaging? Do reluctant speakers ever need to be forced into interaction? Is interaction helpful even if it is with individuals who are not particularly empathetic? And what about those individuals who claim they just learned a new language from watching TV and reading—Didn't they need interaction? The jury is still out on questions like these.

Fluency

Successful language learners have a great deal of language readily accessible in their brains because it has been learned to the point of automaticity. Repeated use of words and phrases has caused them to flow easily, without much thought or strain. But although repetition is a needed feature of language learning, we also know that the repetition needs to be meaningful. For example, repeating "What is your name?" after the teacher ten times is boring and demotivating; but asking ten different people what their names are, while filling out a survey about your classmates on the first day of class is *not* boring, because it is meaningful. The key is to have a lot of repetition, but to get it in a way that is authentic.

I pointed out earlier in this chapter that input should contain no more than 5 percent new language. But when fluency is the goal, we actually want 0 percent new language. In other words, fluency is built by using the new language you already understand, over and over again. And fluency is not limited to speaking. When we have opportunities to hear the same language again and again, with full understanding, listening fluency is built. When listening fluency has not kept pace with language development in the other skills (speaking, reading, and writing), we risk not being able to listen as fast as our interlocutor can talk!

Reading fluency is needed as well. Have you ever wondered why some of the most successful, engaging children's books are full of repetition? (Think, for example, of "Do you like green eggs and ham? *I do not like them, Sam-I-Am!*") Enjoyable repetition in text helps to build reading skills. Writing fluency may also be important. Many of us can quickly compose an email, in our native language, asking if a friend is free to go out for coffee on a certain date. That language easily rolls off our fingertips because we've composed those kinds of sentences repeatedly.

It probably goes without saying that this kind of repeated language—heard, read, or produced—is instrumental in fostering cultural competence along with language acquisition. I remember being taken aback in Kenya and Nigeria when I would get in a car or enter a room and a person's first words to me were "You're welcome," as if I had failed to say "Thank you" for something! But after just a short time, the local use of "You're welcome," used as an American might just say "Welcome," became second nature, and one time I even almost used it back in the States. I had acquired that little cultural piece through meaningful repetition.

While we know for sure that we need to build fluency, we still don't know exactly what this should look like in good second language teaching and learning. For example, is it just as useful to simulate bargaining in a market with a fellow language learner and get repeated use that way, or is more automaticity built if you are actually in the market and bargaining? Can some of the needed repetition come through traditional written exercises? Can fluency come through self-talk, as you repeat language in your mind? No doubt many of these questions are dependent on a variety of factors, including personality. However we do it, a good goal to guide language learning is this: **Learn a little; use a lot**.

Principles of Language Acquisition

Natural sequence
One of the five points in Stephen Krashen's monitor model is that language is learned in a predictable sequence. All of us who have worked at learning a second language know this to be true on some level. For example, when we first begin learning a language we expect to learn things like colors and numbers, not complex verb tenses. We have an intuitive sense that simple nouns and adjectives come before abstract grammar constructions.

At this point, a graphic illustrating how we typically refer to language levels may be helpful. In the language learning trajectory here, we can see five levels, from "beginning" to "advanced." Though individual learners certainly may acquire words and structures here and there that may be out of sequence, in general a learner will progress from beginning to advanced in a somewhat predictable fashion.

Level 1:	Level 2:	Level 3:	Level 4:	Level 5:
Beginning	High beginning	Low intermediate	High intermediate	Advanced

Note: Appendix A provides several different language proficiency scales which contain descriptors of language use at various levels. Your organization may utilize one of these, or a variation of one of them, to document language learning progress.

One frequent cause of lack of progress in language acquisition is the failure to match language content to the learner's level. For example, when we see language learners struggling through a difficult text, looking up many words and failing to grasp the main idea in the process, we see a case of content that is not at the right level for the learners. In another situation, a teacher proceeds through a course book, moving on to new lessons whether previous lessons have been learned or not. In such a case of marching through a curriculum without checking to see if the students are with you, content can quickly become out of sync with actual learner language ability. This can also happen in a self-designed study program if the language learner believes that "more and harder" is better and if he fails to realize that struggling through language tasks significantly above one's current level rarely is helpful in SLA.

But there are cases of content lagging behind learner progress as well. Sometimes this happens because of poorly designed curricula, and other times because teachers choose their own content and teach what they enjoy teaching. I've spoken to English learners in Brazil who have said, "It's the verb *to be* over and over again, every year. I'm sick of studying the verb to be!" A self-styled language program could fall into this trap as well, especially upon reaching an intermediate level. If a learner doesn't conscientiously continue to push language study into that 5 percent of unknown language, language acquisition can stall or stop.

While we all can see the logic of a natural order in language acquisition, it is much less certain what, precisely, that order is. For English learners, we could ask questions such as "Is simple past tense acquired before present continuous?" or "Is adjective word order acquired before compound sentence structures?" We might also consider pragmatics, asking a question such as "Should learners acquire an understanding of when and where it's appropriate to ask a person's age as they learn to form that question in English? Or does that understanding come later, after more interaction with the target language and culture?" Though researchers continue to try to understand the ideal or typical language acquisition sequence, no doubt any such sequence would be impacted by individual and contextual factors.

Language focus

Language acquisition occurs mainly through exposure to and meaningful use of the language. Amid that meaningful use, however, we occasionally need times to *focus on form* (Long 1997), as mentioned above. Such focus might include looking closely at the verb forms or discourse features in a paragraph. It could also involve spending time specifically on learning how to place the tongue and lips to produce a certain sound, then repeating a word list utilizing that sound.

Because this kind of study is more often *overused* than *underused*, it is important to note that all language features do not need to be studied in this way. If a language learner intuitively "gets" a language construction and uses it correctly, then there may never be a need for him to investigate the grammar behind it. Most of us use our native language perfectly well, even though few native speakers can explain the grammar of their native language without specifically studying it. So language focus is not essential for language acquisition. But there are usually parts of the new language that are confusing for adult learners, so actively studying those elements may bring clarity and understanding. The key is to ensure that this kind of study doesn't take over the whole language learning enterprise. It needs to remain only a small part of language acquisition time.

That said, we do know that language learners sometimes begin with many hours—and even years—in "language focus" classrooms. Such is the case in many foreign language courses that consist mostly of grammar, vocabulary, and reading/writing exercises. Interestingly, when given an opportunity to engage in language acquisition through meaningful language use, students coming from these contexts may fare poorly at first. However, once all that grammar and vocabulary begins to be activated through real, meaningful language use, they may do quite well.

The language that was learned passively all those years can become activated—and usable. So there isn't just one way to leverage language focus for the purpose of furthering overall language acquisition.

Stress

As we have seen, Krashen proposed the concept of an "affective filter," which, when elevated due to stress, would hinder learning. Brain research has now confirmed this theory. Bailey and Pransky (2013) suggest that cognitive overload can easily occur in language learning contexts and that this results in stress and reduces acquisition. Other known stressors in language acquisition include expectations of language performance that are beyond the learner's current ability, fears of "getting something wrong" in the classroom, and the sheer mental, physical, and emotional fatigue that goes hand in hand with learning a new language and culture. All of these can raise the affective filter so that the language is not learned effectively.

A caution in utilizing this theory is that stressors can be very personal in nature. While one person may experience stress in a language classroom due to still not understanding a language structure that the teacher has explained several times, another person may be traumatized by going to the market and interacting with locals.

I remember one such time in my Swahili-learning days. I did well on the assignments in class; and thankfully our class time did focus mostly on meaningful and authentic language use. So I probably should have been prepared for the moment when the teacher suddenly announced, "Now, we will go out to the courtyard and you will talk with people there about your families." Though I am not normally shy about speaking with strangers, even in a new language, that sudden assignment terrified and angered me. I knew I hadn't yet learned the phrases well enough to be using them with strangers. I knew I would sound like a babbling infant. I knew I wouldn't be able to communicate well about my family, or ask and understand about the other person's family, which I would very much like to have been able to do.

The activity was as stressful and frustrating as I had imagined it would be. To this day, what I remember most about my Swahili classes is that stressful afternoon. Though my teachers used many other effective activities and teaching strategies, that is the moment that most sticks with me.

A difficulty in navigating the issue of stress in language acquisition is the fact that there are certainly times when language learning is uncomfortable, and successful language learners persevere through those times. It would be impossible to acquire a new language without some stress, because SLA is a challenging and complex endeavor. However … how much stress is too much? I personally think we have probably erred on the side of accepting stress as inevitable and possibly have not worked hard enough to counter some stressors and lower the overall stress levels of language learners and their families. While we don't have a clear picture of exactly how much stress is too much, we do know that stress doesn't add anything of value to language acquisition. If it were possible to remove most stress, language acquisition would be positively impacted.

Time

Our last key word provides the reminder that language acquisition requires nothing if not time. I get annoyed every time I see another blog post or YouTube video making outlandish claims, such as "Learn a language in a month" or "The quick and easy way to learn a language." Run far away from any such sources, because they aren't based in reality.

As we have seen, some estimates place active language learning time at around two thousand hours to reach intermediate to advanced proficiency. Other studies identify one to two years as the time it takes to learn social language and five to seven years as the time it takes to acquire academic or professional language. And even more time may be needed if the target language is vastly different from the native language. Because of the "long-haul" nature of SLA, an unhelpful perspective is to put your life and ministry on hold until you fully acquire the language.

In my research, I discovered misunderstandings on both ends of the time issue. On one hand were those who said they were engaged in full-time language study, but when it came right down to it, they were spending perhaps five to ten hours a week on language learning. This isn't full-time language study, and progress may be slow and frustrating at this rate. Those on the other end of the spectrum, though, feel that they must put in more than forty hours a week on language study. But few people can spend that much time in active language learning for months on end and not suffer burnout. This is especially true if more time in language study means marching through a rigorous curriculum with new language introduced daily.

Just as important as the amount of time devoted to language acquisition is the strategic investment of that time (Brown and Lee 2015). Sometimes a lot of work is done, but it's not the kind of work that is likely to result in real communicative competence. Our next two chapters will highlight what strategic use of language learning time might look like.

Conclusion

If you would like to learn more about the field of SLA, I recommend the following books:

Lessard-Clouston, M. 2017. *Second Language Acquisition Applied to English Language Teaching*. Alexandria, VA: TESOL Press.

Lightbown, P. M., and N. Spada. 2013. *How Languages Are Learned*. Oxford: Oxford University Press.

The first book is a quick and easy read which expands on the theories presented in this chapter. Though its application is in English language teaching, it is an informative book for learners of any language. The second book is more academic in nature, with a focus on studies of learners of many different languages and how this research underpins our current thinking about SLA.

The field of SLA continues to evolve as studies confirm, disprove, or expand on theories, and as we become increasingly aware of how the brain processes a new language. Sending agencies need to stay abreast of these developments in order to ensure that workers have the best possible guidance as they engage in this difficult task. In the remainder of this book I will draw on these concepts as we apply them to the lives and work of those who go abroad to serve in a new language and culture.

Formal Language Learning

JOHN

A lot of different sending organizations are represented in our city, and some of them have started little language schools for their workers. As the leader of our organization here, I've checked out a couple of these options. The problem is, I don't really know what I'm looking for. My own language learning experience was in a bigger school in another city; and to be honest, I hated it. I feel like I mostly learned the language after *I left language school. Was that just me? Do most people like language school, and does it work? I just wish I knew how to pick the best language learning option for our people.*

John is not alone. Listen to enough missionaries talk about their formal language learning experiences and you will find many who either didn't learn as much language as might have been expected, or for whom it was an agonizing experience—despite, perhaps, having made significant progress. On the other hand, there are those who loved language school and who learned the language and culture well for the amount of time spent.

In my adult language learning, I have experienced both of these scenarios. My second Indonesian language learning experience was in a small language school. I am somewhat ashamed to say that because the instruction in that school was so ineffective and demotivating, I didn't persevere longer than a couple of months. As I look back now, I feel a bit sorry for my teacher, who had no training in SLA. What could be worse than having a language teacher as a language student when you have no background in language teaching? My experience of learning Swahili in Tanzania was considerably better. The methods used were good, the teacher had obviously been trained in language teaching methodology, the materials were appropriate, and, for the most part, it was a rewarding experience.

As a language teaching professional, I have been privileged to work in programs in which most of my students experienced success in learning English. I have observed environments in which the teacher took appropriate responsibility for student learning and worked to ensure that the classroom experience was effective and satisfying. So it was in part these different scenarios that drew me to research missionary language acquisition. I wondered why the success I had seen in English learner programs was sometimes absent in language programs for cross-cultural workers.

In this chapter we will consider six areas that affect language program effectiveness: teachers, curriculum, pacing, materials and resources, class instruction, and overall program design. These factors are key to ensuring that participation in the program will result in students acquiring the language, without undo cost to personal and family well-being.

Teachers

Teachers need appropriate qualifications and skills for foreign/second language teaching. Teachers are the single most influential factor in determining language learning success. I have seen highly motivated students become frustrated and tempted to give up because they were being taught by teachers using ineffective and stressful methods. Let's look at some questions that can guide teacher selection.

Has the teacher received training specifically in foreign/second language teaching?

I often hear rationale for using a language teacher along the line of "Maria has a degree in Spanish from a local university," or, a bit better, "Maria has a degree in *teaching* Spanish." However, even the latter doesn't mean that Maria knows how to teach Spanish as a *foreign* language. In fact, it usually means that she is trained to teach Spanish in high school to students who speak Spanish as their native language. The appropriate qualification is that Maria has been trained in teaching *Spanish as a foreign language*. Or if Maria has been trained to teach *English* as a foreign language, that can also work well. Those foreign language teaching skills will transfer well to teaching Spanish as a foreign or second language.

Does the teacher need to be a native speaker of the language?

No! We now have ample research affirming that one does not need to be a native speaker in order to teach a language well. In fact, there are several reasons why *nonnative* speakers who have learned a language well might be the best choice, especially at beginning levels.

1. If choosing between a proficient nonnative speaker who has training in foreign language teaching and a native speaker who does not, the nonnative speaker is probably the much better choice.
2. A nonnative speaker who speaks the same native language as the students and has been through the process of learning the language him/herself, can sometimes be a better guide through the process than a native speaker.
3. A nonnative speaker may speak much more slowly and clearly than a native speaker.

Lest there be any misunderstanding, I am all for employing local teachers who are native speakers of the language being learned. In Indonesia, I developed a program to train local language teachers in foreign language teaching methodologies. Whenever possible, if we can provide the training needed and thus provide employment for locals and interaction with local language speakers, that is a good thing. However, it might not be the *first* thing. It may be best to begin language study with a foreigner who has learned the language well and is well trained in language teaching methods. Then, as a high beginning level is reached, that may be a good time to switch to a local teacher—who is hopefully also well trained in foreign language teaching.

Does the teacher need to speak the language of the students?
No. I have successfully taught many beginning English students whose native language I did not speak. Methodology and curriculum, however, are *critical* in this case. If a teacher is *not* well trained in foreign language teaching methodology, then, at beginning levels, it can be important for the teacher to have at least a low level of proficiency in the student's native language.

There is a downside to this, though. During our first term in Indonesia, our language tutor spent most of the class time telling us cultural tidbits in English. Though it was helpful to learn the culture, we were not learning the language. The appropriate way to address culture learning is to create classes specifically focused on that, and to infuse language learning with culture learning, at appropriate language levels, while using the new language.

Does the teacher need to have experience in teaching a foreign language?
Not necessarily. Sometimes I hear statements such as, "Igor doesn't have any formal training, but he has tutored our missionaries in Russian for ten years." That experience *may* have helped Igor become a good language teacher, but there is certainly no guarantee that it has. What is most important is that Igor uses effective methodology. (See appendix D for some types of activities that are effective for language acquisition.) And no matter how much experience someone has teaching a language, formal training in teaching a foreign language is always helpful.

Curriculum

After the training and effectiveness of teachers, curriculum is the most impactful factor in predicting language learning success, and it must be selected to meet the needs of the learners. Since curriculum is a plan for learning, it should include what is to be learned; and ideally it would also include assessments which will determine the level of learning. Assessments should be measures of actual ability to use the language for real communication, not just paper tests that evaluate passive knowledge of words and grammar.

A curriculum is not a textbook, since language learning should always involve more than a textbook. If the curriculum uses a textbook/workbook, it should not only outline how students will progress through the book, but also what additional learning, activities, and assessments will supplement the book.

There are many different ways of organizing a language curriculum, including these common ones:

- Grammar-based: typically has lessons or units focused on learning grammar points
- Functional: focuses on the functions of language, such as "Purchasing something in a market" and "Making an invitation"
- Theme-based: focuses language learning around major themes, such as family, food, clothing, etc.
- Task-based: arranges the curriculum in terms of tasks that students will complete, such as telling about their families or writing an email

Many curricula and textbooks combine two or more of these elements. For example, my own "English for Life" curriculum (see appendix B), which is adaptable to any language, is broadly organized into themes but utilizes tasks to frame the learning goals. Or a grammar-based curriculum may include in each unit both a grammar goal and a functional goal.

The focus of a language curriculum should be learning and using the language that students need to be able to use. The following points can provide guidance in selecting and evaluating a curriculum:

1. The curriculum and the student's language level must match. Ideally, we learn language through interactions, experiences, and materials in which 95 percent of what we see and hear is *known*, and this allows us to acquire the 5 percent that is new. The curriculum needs to provide materials and activities which respect this incremental language increase. There is little benefit in having a student struggle through materials and grammar concepts that present him with an overwhelming number of new words and structures on a daily basis. This is a recipe for demotivation and failure.

2. A curriculum that is focused mostly on grammar is usually not the best. This is especially true when the grammar materials use decontextualized exercises, such as filling in blanks with correct verb forms in a list of unrelated sentences. While such activities may play a small role in language learning, a much more important task for true language acquisition would be for students to write paragraphs or engage in dialogue using that verb form. We learned in chapter 2 that only 25 percent of language development time should be spent studying *about* the language. The majority of time should be spent actively using the language for real communication. Grammar is normally best incorporated into a curriculum focused on *using* the language, not functioning as the driving force of the curriculum.

3. A system in which the textbook *is* the curriculum is highly suspect! Even the best language textbook should be integrated into an overall plan detailing what will be learned, how language will be practiced and assessed, and what additional activities will contribute to learning. In our English school in Brazil, for example, our overall curriculum consisted of our "English for Life" materials supplemented by limited use of a grammar text, conversation tasks with trained tutors, and additional learning opportunities through "modules" such as cooking or Bible study.

4. A curriculum should have the flexibility to meet the specific needs of the learners. For example, a language student who will be involved in microfinancing will need more financial and business language than most. Similarly, a student who will be teaching in the new language needs to learn not only foundational language but also typical classroom language and norms, such as learning acceptable attention-getting phrases and communicating requirements and expectations.

Pacing

The pace of the instruction must allow for repetition and fluency development. Sometimes an overall curriculum is well designed, but its pacing is too fast. I will address two common problems with pacing, followed by a third which is less common but equally problematic.

Problem 1: Pacing which assumes needed practice will occur outside of class

As we saw in the last chapter, a key to SLA is "Learn a little; use a lot." One misconception, however, is that this "use" should primarily occur outside of class, as learners interact with locals and practice the language they are learning. For many learners, especially at beginning stages, this approach may be much more stressful than helpful. In fact, some of the most heart-wrenching stories I have heard from missionaries involve required outings to use their new language with locals. A small percentage of the population is motivated and eager to do this. These individuals are the natural extroverts—the ones who would probably rather be learning the language out among the people than in a language school anyway. But for many others, this is an unrealistic demand, especially at beginning language levels. I advocate caution for three reasons.

1. Very often, the language form that learners are supposed to practice outside of class is insufficiently taught in the classroom. Teachers forget that learners must not only know what they are supposed to say; they must also have the ability to understand what is said back to them. When the interlocutor's response is not understood, it can be awkward and embarrassing for both, and communication can come to an abrupt halt.

2. The "man on the street" typically doesn't know how to interact with a language learner. It is in the controlled environment of the classroom that appropriate interactions at the learner's level are most likely to take place.

3. Language is acquired when communication is *successful*. Little is accomplished when a required phrase is used with a local, only to have it not be understood or accomplish its intended goal. The demotivation which can result through such interactions may be much more damaging than many language teachers realize.

These cautions do not mean that assignments to go out and use the language with "real people" are never appropriate. But they should be preceded by ample practice time in class. And if at all possible, the language learner should be accompanied by a local assistant, tutor, or cultural guide who can jump in when communication falters, explain to the local interlocutor what the language learner is trying to accomplish, and most of all be empathetic, helpful, and encouraging to the new language user.

The point here is that the pacing of the regular classroom lessons *must* include copious amounts of practice within the lessons themselves. Language teachers need to create engaging and meaningful activities in which students will use, use, use the language they are learning, coming to recognize many potential responses right within the classroom.

Problem 2: Pacing which moves through instruction as fast as students can "get it"

Another common misconception of SLA is that it is mostly about understanding the words and structures of the language. In reality, nothing could be further from the truth. We may be able to move through a grammar book fairly swiftly, understanding the structures and using them correctly in fill-in-the-blank exercises. This does *not* mean, however, that we can use all this language in real communicative contexts. In fact, it has been noted that the very students who excel in grammar study may struggle the most in real communication requiring that very same grammar.

This was the case with my mother, whose story I recounted in chapter 1. She excelled in grammar study—only to realize later that she couldn't communicate very well with regular people. Rather than proceeding as quickly as students can understand how the language is put together, language instruction should proceed as quickly as students can feel comfortable using it fluently and with reasonable accuracy for real communication, with a variety of interlocutors.

Problem 3: Pacing which moves too slowly
It is far more common to hear stories of pacing that is too fast as opposed to pacing that is too slow. However, when the latter does occur, it is equally damaging to language acquisition. When pacing doesn't progress quickly enough, here are the typical culprits:

- A language teacher has not been trained well for all language levels and therefore reverts to the comfort of teaching lower-level concepts and language. This may happen in a program or class where needed assessment and evaluation measures are lacking, resulting in the teacher not knowing what the student already knows and what he still needs to learn. Note that this may also be a problem of *curriculum*, and not necessarily just one of pacing.

- A language teacher is tied to the curriculum and pacing of the book, thus failing to continually assess a student's level of language proficiency and to gear instruction to real learning needs. Such a teacher may, for example, neglect to routinely begin new lessons by assessing whether or not the students already know the language, and as a result may not skip lessons that aren't needed.

- A language class is made up of multiple levels, and the needs of all levels are not being met. It *is* possible to teach multilevel classes well. (See comments below, under "Class Instruction.") However, a high level of teacher skill and training are needed, and too often teachers address the needs of the students in the middle, neglecting the needs of those at the lower and upper ends of proficiency.

Materials

Instructional materials must be leveled appropriately and be engaging, with meaningful repetition. Books, workbooks, audio recordings, computer software, online programs and apps all have the potential to contribute positively to both language acquisition and motivation. Technology now provides more resources for developing oral language, and cutting-edge applications can integrate the latest in language learning theory, such as "timed repetitions." That said, many formal language study settings still use the traditional materials of textbooks and workbooks. Whether or not resources include modern technology, here are a few key principles to keep in mind:

Principle 1: Materials need to be at the learner's level

As we have learned, we can envision the "learner's level" as language that is 95 percent known or understood. When materials are at the correct level, the learner's continual experience of success and ability to progress through the materials provides significant motivation for continuing on with SLA.

How can we know if material is at the learner's level? One quick and easy assessment is to select a one-hundred-word passage; have the learner read the passage, underlining all the words she doesn't know. If she underlines more than five words, the passage may be too difficult. The same strategy could be used with an oral dialogue that has been transcribed.

Probably the most straightforward way to know if material is at the right level is to listen to the learner. If learners are aware that material which is too difficult for them will not accelerate their language acquisition, they will be more likely to speak up when something seems too hard and they need material at a lower level.

Principle 2: Materials should be engaging and age appropriate

All learning is most effective when learners are genuinely interested in the content. This is especially true for language acquisition. A student who loves to cook will likely be much more motivated by course materials providing recipes in the target language than by readings about historical events in the country. A student who loves history, on the other hand, will likely be inspired by such readings. In any given language class, students will have different interests. This is why the best course materials and curricula provide some choice in readings and activities. While not every student needs to find every reading or activity exciting, the more a teacher can utilize materials which the majority of the students find interesting, the better.

Stories and dialogues used in language learning materials should be written in interesting, authentic language. A familiar criticism of textbook dialogues is that they don't reflect how people actually talk. Teachers need to be aware of this tendency and willing to rewrite dialogues as needed. A similar complaint is that readings in language texts are dry and boring. Even articles about historical events can be written in engaging ways, and a good textbook will reflect this value.

Finally, materials should be age appropriate. Sometimes older beginning language learners, unfortunately, are given materials designed for young children. Even beginning language learners need materials that are appealing to their age group, both visually and thematically.

Principle 3: Materials should be user friendly

Language materials vary considerably from country to country. The presentation, types of activities, sequencing of language items, and more might not look like our high-school Spanish textbooks. Though a person entering a new language and culture needs to be open to course materials which are presented differently, here are some basic ingredients which characterize user-friendly language learning materials across cultures:

- Spaces to write in answers are easily recognizable as "blanks," and large enough to accommodate the answers. Some cultures use straight lines. Some use a sequence of dots. Students need to be able to recognize either of these as a "blank" and be able to fit their answer into it.
- Text is large enough to read without straining. In some countries I have seen very small fonts used in learning materials. This may be due to a need to conserve paper and reduce costs. Many language learners, however, would prefer to pay a little more for materials in a larger font.
- Lesson topics and new language are clearly provided at the beginning of the chapter. The target learning goals are clear.
- Materials provide clear definitions and example sentences of new words, through glosses on the side or glossaries in the back.
- Visuals are sufficient and easy to interpret.

Principle 4: Materials should provide meaningful repetition

Though some of the repetition needed to develop fluency and automaticity should occur through oral interactions in the classroom that are not driven by the text, the more a course text *does* provide meaningful repetition and review, the greater the likelihood of students getting enough practice. For example, course materials could include survey tasks in which students go around the room asking questions of the other students in order to fill in a survey form. This provides excellent, authentic repetitive language use.

Good course materials might also include games, songs, and directions for oral tasks. In fact, if teachers aren't well trained in SLA, textbooks and workbooks play a significant role in ensuring that there is sufficient practice embedded in the lessons, and that this practice is meaningful.

Principle 5: Materials should be all or mostly in the target language— the language being learned

If the "5 percent new language" rule is followed, it is usually possible to keep the learning materials all in the target language. Stock textbook phrases such as

"Vocabulary," "Fill in the blank," "Read and answer the questions," and "Match words in A and B" can certainly be learned quickly and can be provided only in the target language. If translation is needed for instructions, it can be given orally in the class and may not need to appear in the textbook. In situations in which learners come from several different native-language backgrounds, it is especially important to keep all of the text in the target language.

Class Instruction

Instruction should include diverse activities, including pair and group activities in which students engage in meaningful speech. Some language learners believe that one-on-one tutoring is most effective for language acquisition. In some contexts this is the only option, and such tutoring scenarios will be addressed in chapter 4. Where group classroom instruction is available, however, it provides the best language learning environment for most language learners. Here is why:

1. Class instruction can provide a lot of pair and small group interaction. One key ingredient for acquiring a language is having many opportunities to use it. However, this use is often most effective when interlocutors are at similar levels. Some fear that using the new language with another person at their same language level will result in learning incorrect language, as they hear the other person's errors. This has not been shown to be the case, however. Conversing with fellow learners does *not* increase the potential of long-term errors. Rather, it provides input at the learner's appropriate level, at the speed and with the language that is needed at that level. In other words, a fellow language learner can be the very *best* interlocutor!

2. Class instruction can provide fun and engaging activities such as games, surveys, interviews, songs and chants, group projects, and more. Many more activity types are possible with a group than in one-on-one instruction. Many such activities increase a sense of community, build relationships, provide for diverse ways to engage with the new language, and ultimately lower stress levels considerably.

3. Class instruction lessens the stress of having to speak all the time. A tutoring situation consists of just the teacher, who is usually a native speaker of the language, and the student. In this kind of setting communication is continuous, and a person's limit for interacting in the new language is more quickly reached. At this point, either the session is finished, or the talk lapses into the learner's native language, or the tutor presses on—increasing anxiety and stress in the learner. In a classroom setting, where several students are taking turns talking and being the center of attention, a learner has continual mini-breaks in language effort. This can result in the ability to stay engaged for a longer period of time, ultimately resulting in more successful language acquisition with less stress.

There are, of course, classroom environments which are quite challenging. Here are some common issues faced in classroom instruction, and suggestions for minimizing difficulties:

Multilevel classes

Let's first define what is meant by a "multilevel" class. In any language classroom, no two learners will be at exactly the same level or know all the same language. This is not a problem when learners are at *similar* places in their language development. For example, if we have two learners at a beginning level, one might know numbers 1–10 already and one might just be learning those numbers. But both are learning to formulate simple sentences, and both can benefit from an activity involving stating the ages of their children. A true multilevel class, on the other hand, is one in which individuals are at quite different levels. If you recall the five levels of language proficiency outlined in chapter 2, a multilevel class consists of a level 1 student in the same class with a level 3 student, or a level 3 student in a class with a student at level 5.

These conditions are not ideal, and private tutoring may be more beneficial. Still, a capable teacher *can* utilize some specific strategies for ensuring that students are able to make language gains in a multilevel classroom environment. Such strategies include:

- *Differentiation of some materials and tasks.* This means that students don't do all the same things in class. For example, the class topic might be developing the language used in a restaurant. Lower-level students might be learning simple phrases to order food and ask for the bill. Higher-level students, on the other hand, might be tasked with writing a dialogue for explaining an allergy to a server and asking what ingredients are in several of the menu items.

- *Integration of different levels in the same activity, but with different goals.* For example, learners might be sharing about their families. Beginners might just be learning the words and structures. Intermediate learners, on the other hand, could use that activity to develop fluency, perhaps even timing their responses.

- *Helping learners to understand the different levels and needs in the room.* Doing so can help foster a climate of support and encouragement for all.

It is typically easier to combine levels at higher proficiencies. For example, level 3 and level 5 students might be able to work on similar projects and tasks, with level 5 students producing more complex language than level 3 students. On the other hand, it can be quite difficult to have raw beginners, those who are just starting out in learning the language, in the same classroom with those just a little higher, at level 2. The needs of beginners are quite different, as they have attained no language and need to learn basic word sets and simple structures before they can begin to interact. If at all possible, low beginning language learners shouldn't be in classes with those who are more advanced.

For more information on language instruction in multilevel classes, I recommend *Mixed-Ability Teaching*, by Edmund Dudley and Erika Osvath (Oxford, 2016); and *Teaching Multilevel Classes in ESL*, by Jill Bell (Pippin Publishing, 2004).

Climate of competition

Some classes develop a climate of competition rather than of collaboration and support. Unfortunately, this can occur even in a classroom full of missionaries! Underlying competition between members of the same organization might already exist, as well as subtle competition between spouses. (This, and other family well-being issues, will be addressed more extensively in chapter 7).

If this is the case, the solution isn't to abandon the class but to correct attitudes. Part of a teacher's mandate is to create a positive climate in the classroom. The teacher needs to confront overt disrespectful behavior such as laughing at or belittling another student, either during class or by talking with the offender after class. Teachers can also preempt some competitive behavior at the beginning of a course by emphasizing the positive effect of students collaborating with each other as they learn. But in many missionary language learning contexts, the teacher may not feel that she has the authority to correct such behaviors. It then becomes important for students to monitor themselves and each other and work together toward a healthy classroom learning environment. This is uncomfortable and hard, but necessary.

Coping with a teacher's lack of training

If the teacher is not well trained in language teaching, navigating that deficit can be more difficult in a classroom context than in a one-on-one context. In a tutoring situation, the learner can usually talk with the teacher about what he or she needs and wants from the tutoring session and have a voice in what is studied. In a classroom situation, this can be more difficult. Students may not feel that they have the right to suggest alternative materials or methods. I believe students *do* have the right, and in fact a mandate, to speak up. Chapter 4 provides more direction on how to navigate poor language instruction in a positive way.

There are usually ways to maximize the benefits of classroom instruction, while minimizing the drawbacks. This being the case, classroom instruction often provides the most ideal language learning context for many people.

Program

The overall language program needs to take into consideration the whole person, family, and community. In evaluating a language *program*, we look at features beyond the classroom experience, such as these:

- The type of assessment used and the format in which students are provided with feedback on their learning. Do they receive letter or number grades? If so, how do these help them in their learning?
- School/program policies and procedures. If a student is having difficulty in a class, does he know who to talk to? How will the issue be resolved?
- Additional support provided for language learning. Is there a library? Are there media and technology resources?
- Homework. Does the program or school have a well-informed homework policy? Does the policy take into consideration realities in regard to family obligations and the considerable time it can take to learn to live in a new country? Is the policy followed by the teachers?
- Additional requirements, such as using the language outside the classroom. Are these requirements appropriate for the learner's level? Do they increase motivation or do they cause undue stress? Has the community where the language will be practiced been informed and coached in their role?
- Timing of classes and other requirements. Does the schedule mesh well with students' other obligations and realities?

Some of the greatest challenges in the many language learning stories I have heard came not from the language learning classroom itself, but from programmatic issues such as too much homework, stressful and unhelpful tests, and schedules preventing sufficient family time. All of these are important considerations in the selection of a language course or program.

Conclusion

My hope is that the information in this chapter can help mission leaders like John, whose story introduced the chapter. By knowing more about the areas of teacher preparedness, curriculum, pacing, materials and resources, class instruction, and overall program design, someone like John can make informed decisions as to which school or course would be best for those joining his team. And if he is unable to find an ideal language learning program, he is equipped to provide suggestions to a willing school (perhaps by recommending this book) to help them improve their effectiveness.

Informal Language Learning

AMY

The language we're learning is not exactly an obscure one—it's spoken by thousands of people in the area where we're going. Still, there doesn't seem to be any formal language program to study this language. So I'm wondering what our best options are. Should we hire a tutor who maybe has taught English and can transfer those skills to teaching us the local language? Should we just work on it on our own, getting a language helper? I've heard people suggest different things, and I just don't know how to choose the best option.

Amy's questions are shared by many. When I began to investigate missionary language acquisition, after having been a language teacher for many years, I was struck by the predominant, and almost exclusive, emphasis on the role of the *learner* in the language acquisition endeavor within missionary circles. As a language teacher, I had always borne a good part of the responsibility for my students' language acquisition. I felt that if my students weren't acquiring English, that meant that I, the *teacher*, needed to change something. So placing the full burden of language acquisition on the shoulders of the language *learner* was a new perspective for me.

One of the earliest learner-driven language acquisition approaches used by missionaries was the LAMP method: "Language Acquisition Made Practical." It emphasized memorizing dialogues and phrases and using them frequently. Pioneered by Tom and Betty Sue Brewster in the 1970s, the LAMP method took hold in the missionary community, and it is still recommended by many today for some of its down-to-earth and practical features, such as the motto we saw in chapter 2: "Learn a little; use a lot."

More recently, Greg Thomson developed the "Growing Participator Approach," or GPA. Learners move through a six-phase program in which they "grow" in "participating" in the local language and culture. The GPA has proved to be a helpful guide for many self-directed language learners and is also utilized in some formal language study programs.

My goal in this chapter is not to evaluate these approaches and offer recommendations or to present another packaged "method" or "approach" for self-directed language study. Rather, my aim is to provide foundational understanding that can inform and direct learner-driven choices regarding language study. After clarifying some terminology, we will consider two approaches to informal language study: utilizing a tutor and utilizing a language helper. Next I will provide a list of things to consider as you guide your own learning, followed by a section about continuing language learning after formal language study. The chapter will conclude with a list of questions to walk you through the process of selecting the best language learning scheme for you.

Terminology

Terms related to language study are used differently by different people, so here is how I am using the following terms:

- *"Informal" Language Learning:* In my usage in this book, "informal" does not mean "unplanned." In fact, successful language study is normally well planned. It takes many hours of disciplined engagement to learn a language. The term "informal" here is used in contrast with a "formal" language course or program, which was outlined in chapter 3.

- *Tutor:* A language tutor is a language teacher who teaches a class of one. Ideally, the tutor is trained in teaching a second or foreign language. We saw in chapter 3 that a language teacher doesn't need to be a native speaker in order to be effective, and the same is true of a language tutor. A nonnative speaker of the target language can be very effective, and sometimes may even preferable over a native speaker, especially if the nonnative speaker is trained in foreign language teaching and the native speaker is not.

- *Language Helper:* This term usually refers to someone who models the target language for the language learner. In contexts where an obscure language is being learned, for example, a language helper serves as the source of the language, providing words and structures prompted by the language learner. Even when the language being learned is more widely used, a language learner might prefer learning the language informally, assisted by a language helper, or might engage in this kind of ongoing learning subsequent to formal study. A language helper is not a language teacher and is normally a native speaker of the target language.

- *Language Coach:* A language coach neither teaches the language nor is the source of the language for the learner, but rather provides support in the language learning process. A language coach is often someone from the language learner's culture and language—someone who can provide a listening ear, and sometimes also guidance and suggestions. The language coach may or may not have learned the same language the language student is learning, but should be someone who has successfully learned a language as an adult, and who has a good grasp of second language acquisition theory, research, and methods.

Two Approaches to Informal Language Study

In this section I will address informal language study first through tutoring and then through self-directed study utilizing a language helper.

A tutoring arrangement

When engaging in language learning through a planned tutoring arrangement, most of the same criteria introduced in chapter 3 are applicable. The tutor should be a teacher who is well trained in teaching a second or foreign language. The *curriculum* should meet learner needs and be focused on meaningful communication. Pacing is often easier to tailor to the student's needs and realities in a one-on-one setting. However, the tendency with a tutoring arrangement may be to allow a slower than ideal pace, making it difficult to reach long-term goals. *Materials* should be leveled appropriately and provide meaningful tasks in the target language. Finally, the formal *program* of study needs to take into consideration the student's needs and realities.

A tutoring arrangement could be very similar to a formal classroom learning environment, only without the other students. Some language schools have a formal program, but the classes just happen to be classes of one. In this situation, the school likely has a curriculum and materials, just as a larger program or school would.

In other situations, the language learner or his agency hires a tutor. In this case, the tutor may or may not have a prepared curriculum and materials. If no curriculum is in place, then the tutoring arrangement may become more like "Guiding your own learning" below.

The tutor in a tutoring arrangement often speaks some English, so without the pressure of a classroom atmosphere and other students to keep the lessons on track, class time can readily lapse into conversations in English. Sometimes the tutor may legitimately be explaining grammar or culture in English, but it's easy for such strategies to stretch into prolonged times of English use, which is generally not the goal of the language class. While it isn't appropriate to ban the native language, since it can be a helpful tool in learning a new language, it's also important to stay focused on the language acquisition goal and ensure that the majority of each lesson takes place *in* the target language, at the learner's language proficiency level.

Assistance from a language helper
In some contexts, usually in which the language being learned isn't widely spoken, there is no possibility of having a trained language teacher or tutor and no expectation of a prepared curriculum or materials. Instead it is understood from the outset that upon arrival in the new context, the language learner will look for a suitable language helper—someone who can supply the words and phrases of the new language and who will empathetically engage with the language learner as she attempts to use the new language. Agencies which send workers into these types of environments may have suggested protocols and resources for language study with a language helper. Whether or not the agency provides guidance, the points below can be helpful in planning your course of study.

Guiding Your Own Learning

Several situations may result in a language learner guiding his or her own learning. Perhaps "formal study" was envisioned, but it turns out not to be as "formal" as expected. Or maybe a hired tutor shows up on the first day and asks, "What do you want to learn?" rather than bringing with him a textbook and curriculum. Or maybe you left your home country already expecting to direct your own learning, working with a language helper. Whatever the circumstances, language learners sometimes play at least some role in directing their own learning. When this is the case, the following guidance may prove to be useful.

1. **Adopt a curriculum.** Even if it is a very simple one, having the guidance of a curriculum can help to keep learning sessions on track. My "English for Life" task-based curriculum, in appendix B, provides a simple checklist of tasks to be able to accomplish in the target language; and it can easily be adapted to any language. Other lists of language functions, grammar forms, and communicative tasks can be found online.
2. **Set realistic and specific goals.** "Be able to preach in the target language within six months" is probably not realistic! And a goal such as "Be able to communicate with neighbors" is not specific enough. On the other hand,

"Be able to tell someone the number and ages of my children within two weeks" might be a very appropriate goal. If you're using a textbook, don't just have book-completion goals, such as "Complete chapter 1 in two weeks." Rather, look at the language that you are learning to use in chapter 1 and create a goal to use that language. For example, if chapter 1 includes words about food, you might set a goal of being able to write your shopping lists in the new language within one week and to ask for fruits and vegetables by name in the market within two weeks.

3. **Focus on meaningful language use.** The goal in learning a new language is to be able to *use* that language for authentic, meaningful communication. If your tutor or language helper has not studied Second Language Acquisition (SLA), they may believe that grammar exercises or workbooks should take a central role in the language lesson. However, such activities should only be used in a supporting role. The main activity to engage in both in and out of class is meaningful language use. Here are some examples of how that might work:

   - To learn past verb forms, practice telling your tutor or helper what you did yesterday, last week, etc. Some grammar pages eliciting past verb forms could play a supporting role in equipping you for this task, but the task of narrating your activities and being able to comprehend your helper's past activities, should be the main focus.

   - To learn how to state the time, ask your helper about his/her daily schedule and tell your helper about your schedule. Again, a worksheet in which you look at a clock and fill in time phrases could be a helpful step toward the communicative goal, but actual communication about real-life situations is the much more important task.

   - To learn appropriate words, phrases, and customs when attending a funeral, a written dialogue may be a useful starting point. But the end task should be several role-plays in class, in which you encounter possible funeral scenarios and conditions and attempt to communicate appropriately with your tutor or helper in those scenarios.

   The place of a grammar book, a language textbook with vocabulary and dialogues, and worksheets is always in a supporting role. Keep real, meaningful communication as the main goal.

4. **Create learning aids.** Most language learners know the value of labeling items around the house, and some enjoy working with flashcards. But there are many other types of learning aids which can also be made by learners, and which can contribute to language acquisition. For example, learners can create their own games, music, chants, recipes, graphic organizers,

and much more. Anything that a language teacher might create for her class, a language student could create with the assistance of a tutor or language helper. Some ideas for learning aids and activities can be found in appendix E.

5. **Review and recycle.** In well-designed language textbooks, opportunities to use previously learned language are built into the curriculum. When guiding your own learning, continued use of the language you have already learned needs to be thoughtfully integrated into language study. The notion of "two steps forward, one step back" can provide useful direction here. If every third lesson is comprised of going back and using language forms from a previous lesson, unit, or topic rather than moving forward, sufficient opportunity will be provided to solidify and build fluency in that language, moving it into long-term, easily accessible, memory.

A caution: Many tutors and helpers may feel that this isn't necessary! They may want to just move on, saying "You already know this!" What they don't understand is that your current proficiency in using language that has been recently learned may not yet be fluent and may not yet have reached the point of automaticity. Insist on the review. It will stand you in good stead in the long run.

6. **Build in assessment.** One of the most difficult things to do on your own is to assess your progress. Many language self-assessment systems are worded quite loosely, and language learners have been known to either overrate or underrate themselves in comparison to the assessment of a language professional. Some assessments are also very broad, failing to tease apart differences in proficiency in the various domains (reading, writing, speaking, and listening) and in various topics and themes (e.g., highly proficient in language about food, but not able to hold a conversation about health).

Despite these potential limitations, self-assessment can provide a useful snapshot of your progress and is certainly better than no assessment at all. Your assessment system should be aligned with whatever curriculum you are using. You could use a checklist to indicate when you feel comfortable and successful in a given communicative task, perhaps supported by artifacts in a portfolio. The "English for Life" system in appendix B provides this kind of checklist, utilizing "Can do" statements showing what you *can do* in the new language. Such a checklist can be a component of an assessment system, showing your progress in your perceived ability to engage in various language tasks.

One difficulty you may encounter is knowing how to assess your accuracy. For example, you might be successful in a communication task but are using an incorrect grammar form. One way to include accuracy in assessment of spoken language is to engage in a conversational task with your tutor or helper. Record the conversation. Later, listen to it with your helper, asking her to identify each error. Calculate the number of words you spoke (there are computer programs which can transcribe and count the words in an oral excerpt) relative to the number of errors, and turn this into an accuracy percentage. For example, you might find that you have 70 percent accuracy in that particular language task. You might decide you want to work on some specific errors to improve your accuracy. A few weeks later you might decide to assess yourself on the same language task again. If you have 90 percent accuracy the second time around, you have obviously made progress. Keeping a log of such tests and retests and the progress you have made is one way to document your language learning. You could work with the helper further to separate out different types of errors, such as those in pronunciation, grammar, and word use. You may decide, for example, that your pronunciation errors are minimal and don't impede understanding, but that you really need to work on some grammatical constructions.

The purpose of assessment is to provide a record of what you have achieved along with discovering where you still need more work. Regular use of techniques like those above can achieve both of those purposes.

When working with a language tutor, one hurdle you may face is your tutor's belief that a formal, written test is the best and most legitimate form of assessment. However, formal tests are of very limited value in language acquisition. At beginning levels, simple quizzes allowing you to see if you are able to match words to their pictures, for example, could be useful and motivating. Still, doing well on such a quiz is fairly useless if you cannot recall the name of an item you are looking for in a real market during a real conversation. So authentic assessments that gauge your ability to use new language in a real, communicative context are almost always the most valid.

Continuing Your Learning after Formal Study

You may recall my parents' Portuguese language study experiences. My dad pretty much began his language acquisition *after* his year of formal language study, having acquired very little in the formal language school program. My mom felt that she "learned" well in language school, and had the grades to prove it. But when she landed in a real Brazilian community, far from the elite Portuguese of language school, she, too, could not communicate with the locals. Both of my parents essentially had to learn to communicate with real people in Portuguese after leaving language school, once they were immersed in a context where their very lives (and mine) depended upon it!

Though language learning programs have improved in many places and today's language learners hopefully do acquire communication skills during their formal language schooling, the reality is that most language courses are only a year in length, and we know that learning a language to an advanced level takes five to seven years (Collier 1989). This means that *every* language learner will need to continue to learn the language after formal language studies have ended. How should language learners go about this task? Here are some ways forward:

1. **Establish your long-term goals in the domains of reading, writing, speaking, and listening.** You may need to have strong conversation skills in order to develop friendships to a deep and lasting level, but you may not need reading and writing skills beyond an intermediate level. Or you may need strong reading and writing skills because you need to be able to read and write reports for a seminary board in the local language, and you might also need advanced oral skills in order to preach and teach. In addition, you may need specific skills in any of the domains. For example, perhaps you need to be able to fill out government forms. Or maybe you will assist in a clinic and need precise medical vocabulary. The point is to identify the specific areas in which you need to develop local language skills in order to be effective where God has placed you.

2. **Identify resources you will need in order to achieve these goals.** Will you need ongoing help from a language tutor or helper? Or will your budding relationships with those you are ministering with or to suffice? Can you make progress working on your own with the aid of a book, website, or app?

3. **Identify the types of activities you will engage in to achieve your goals.** For example, will you download some government forms from a website, practice filling them out, and then show them to a language helper who will check them for accuracy? Will you prepare a mini-lecture on an academic topic and give it to a friend, asking her to provide feedback on your grammar and pronunciation? Be creative. You may want to return to the "Language Learning Resources" in appendix E and adapt them for your ongoing learning. For example, a medical technician might label medical instruments. Someone who will deal a lot with government agencies might design a "government agency board game" designed to elicit the language and understanding that might be needed when interacting with various government agencies, and then play the game with a language helper.

4. **Identify two to three weekly language study times in your schedule.** Block out these times for regular language study. Also plan out the

specific activities you will engage in week to week to help your language development, along with the resources you will need in order to do these activities. Having an accountability partner, perhaps a coworker, who will check on you and hold you to your schedule can be helpful as well. Or this role might be filled with a language coach assigned by your organization.

5. **Periodically revisit your goals, resources, activities, and language study times.** Nothing is more certain than change, and this is true of language study also. Perhaps your long-term goals will change when you are given a new ministry assignment. Or perhaps a resource that you thought would be helpful is not, and you need to find something different. Don't let such changes derail your long-term language study. Adapt and change ... but *don't neglect your long-term language study.*

Choosing the Best Language Learning Fit for YOU

In this chapter and the previous one we learned about both formal and informal ways to learn a language, along with various models of language study within each. What is right for you and your family? Here are some questions that may help guide your decision-making:

1. Is a reputable, effective formal language school or program a viable option? If so, **choose this!** If not, read on.
2. Is a well-trained, highly effective language tutor, using a proven curriculum, an option? If so, **choose this!** If not, read on.
3. Are either of these options available:
   - A formal language school lacking a clearly effective track record?
   - A language tutor with a good curriculum but lacking training?

   If so, check out both. Do "test classes" to see which might be the best fit for your personality and preferences. **Choose one of these.**
4. If none of the above options is available, you will be navigating your own learning process. Use the guidance in this chapter, and throughout this book, to help you.

Conclusion

One of my father's favorite sayings was "Where God guides, he provides." Though my dad was usually referring to finances, the saying is apt for language learning as well. I don't believe God calls his workers to any location only to leave them stranded without a viable means to learn the language of those whom they are serving. God will make a way to learn the language no matter where you are, no matter who you are, and no matter what circumstances you find yourself in.

Children's Language & Educational Needs

LORI

What I guess we didn't count on was how hard it would be for the kids. We kind of thought they would learn the language just by being here. We expected that at least our youngest would play with the local kids, but it seems like unless I am there with an organized activity, the interaction just doesn't happen. And the ones who are already in school hardly hear any of the language at all, because their school day is almost entirely in English. The two times a week that they actually do get thirty minutes of instruction in the language just turns them off more, because the teachers are either very boring or way too unrealistic in their expectations. And the very hardest part of our week is church on Sunday. We came here with visions of our family participating together in ministry at the church ... but now our kids really dread Sunday mornings, and I don't know how to change that.

Lori's realization that children don't just automatically acquire the language of their new country takes many missionary families by surprise. Because the myth that children learn language easily and effortlessly is so predominant, insufficient attention is often given to the children's language acquisition, by both mission agencies and missionaries. *The failure to understand the reality that the family's ministry will be hugely impacted if the children don't integrate well into the language and culture, and the resulting lack of attention given to children's language learning poses a significant threat to missionary effectiveness and longevity.* It also poses a threat to MK identity and well-being later in life. As adults, MKs may feel a sense of shame if they spent many years in a country and yet never became fluent in the language. They frequently feel that this indicates failure on their part. In reality, though, it is the adults who were responsible for helping them learn the language who are most often to blame for this sense of failure. Both parents and mission organization leaders must ensure that MKs are provided adequate opportunities to acquire the language of the country they grow up in.

What do missionaries and mission agencies need to understand about the language acquisition of MKs, besides the fact that it is very important and should be prioritized? In this chapter, we will first recap what we have learned about second language acquisition in previous chapters, with specific applications to childhood second language acquisition. Next we will consider the three most common educational options for MKs, and look at each through the lens of language acquisition potential. I will then address the ministry aspect of missionary life, focusing on issues and perspectives about the involvement of children in ministry. I will pull all of this together into a short list of priorities to help chart the best course for MK education and language acquisition. Lastly, I will provide some additional information for those who have the possibility of raising their children bilingually, with two first languages.

Childhood Second Language Acquisition

An internet search of "childhood language acquisition" brings up a plethora of information, which can be difficult to sort through and has often been misunderstood and misapplied. Two significant issues typically cloud understanding on this topic. First, we need to know whether we are talking about *first* or *second* language acquisition. And second, we need to look at particular age ranges, rather than "childhood" as a whole.

First and second language acquisition

A child acquires his first, or native, language as a natural part of his development. Basic acquisition of one's first language happens from before birth to three to five years of age. Babies receive a tremendous amount of oral language input, beginning in the womb, before they begin to babble and reproduce some of the sounds they hear. Research by Kuhl (2010) suggests that by the time babies are around ten months old they begin to filter out sounds not represented by the native language, or languages, they are hearing. This helps explain the reality that we reproduce the sounds in our native language perfectly, while we may struggle to produce foreign sounds in a new language later in life.

A child can have two native languages. Called *simultaneous bilingualism*, this occurs when caregivers speak to the child using two languages. A typical scenario for simultaneous bilingualism is when the parents have two different native languages, and they each use their own language with the child. A child can also develop two first languages by learning one from another caregiver, such as a grandparent or a nanny, and the other from the child's parents. However, it is suggested that a child will *not* develop native language ability in any language that comprises less than 30 percent of total language input (Genesee 2007, 6). For example, imagine a child who visits grandparents once a week and they speak to the child in a different language. The child will not develop that language as a native language, because of insufficient input. Once a week is just not enough. But when there is sufficient input, acquiring two native languages is obviously a very attractive way to become bilingual! For parents who want to pursue this goal for their children, see the additional information at the end of this chapter.

We say that a child is learning a new language as a *second* language if the first/native language is already well established, usually somewhere between the ages of three and five. We call this *sequential* bilingualism. However, the experience and outcome of acquiring a second language in childhood will vary tremendously according to context. The amount of exposure to the new language, the type of exposure, and the circumstances and need for using the new language will all have a significant impact on the proficiency achieved in the new language. For example, a Vietnamese child adopted into an American, English-speaking home at age three will likely lose his initial native language, Vietnamese, fairly quickly, and replace it with the new "native" language of English. Similarly, if a child has spoken only Spanish until going to kindergarten, but the school is fully in English, English may become that child's much stronger language within a few years. We would hope that both of these children would be able to retain their initial native language while developing the new language of English. But, depending on resources and context, that may or may not be possible.

Second language acquisition at different ages
In this section we will look at five issues that are central to discussions regarding age and second language acquisition: (1) learning versus acquisition: (2) native-like production; (3) methodology; (4) motivation; and (5) affective factors. In each topic, I will focus on differences for children of different ages.

Learning versus Acquisition
As I mentioned in chapter 2, there is a difference between "acquiring" and "learning" a new language. Though we use the term "language learning" colloquially to include any type of language acquisition, in this section we will

return to Krashen's (1981) distinctions between *acquisition*, or "picking up" a new language through exposure, and *formal learning*, which refers to learning grammar rules, memorizing vocabulary words, etc.

It is fairly obvious that the younger the child, the more the focus should be on *acquiring* language. Songs, chants, games, informal and non-stressful dialogue occurring naturally in task-based instruction—are all key ways in which young children acquire a new language through exposure and repetitive, engaging use. What may be less obvious is that older children, and even adults, benefit from these same strategies! While there may be a barrier to overcome in the perception that these activities are too "childish," older learners who engage in these types of activities usually *do* find that they are effective for language acquisition.

Where *learning* is concerned, the younger the child, the less appropriate is a focus on learning, such as memorization of words, spellings, and grammar rules. I am often asked, "At what age should we begin teaching grammar rules?" I usually respond, "Only when it is helpful."

Grammar is abstract, so children in lower elementary school aren't developmentally ready for discussions about grammar. Some very limited grammar study, especially if done through discovery and student-centered learning, can be helpful for older children. For example, a fourth-grade teacher of English learners created a lesson to help her students discover the three different pronunciations of "ed" in English. The children were excited to discover these pronunciation rule as they worked in small groups, creating and testing hypotheses. This kind of grammar instruction develops critical thinking and engages learners in exploring the new language.

Ultimately, the rule of thumb should be that if *acquisition* is taking place without the direct instruction that comprises *learning*, we should continue to avoid direct vocabulary and grammar instruction, especially if students are passive receivers of that instruction. For example, if a child is able to *acquire* correct verb tense forms through exposure, there is no need to memorize grammar rules governing those forms. In the teen years and beyond, a limited focus on learning *about* the new language can be helpful. Older students have the ability to apply this learning as they engage in *acquisition* tasks, and this conscious application of learned rules can benefit the acquisition process.

A final note is that in the teen years and beyond, the study of linguistics *can* be very beneficial. Learning not only about one's native language and the language one is learning, but learning broad concepts about languages in general, is both fascinating and motivating. There have been many initiatives to introduce linguistics as a core high school subject, replacing some of the outdated English grammar instruction that is still currently common. I heartily support these efforts!

Native-like production

As we have already seen, young children do have an ability that older language learners may not have to hear and reproduce new sounds. This means that the younger the language learner, the greater the likelihood of achieving "native-like" pronunciation. And native-like skill is not limited to sounds. Native speaker language proficiency is also evidenced in some grammatical constructions, idiomatic language use, and other language features.

It has long been thought that the window for achieving native-like language usage closes fairly early—some claimed by age seven, others by puberty. However, more recent and much more comprehensive research by Hartshorne, Tenenbaum, and Pinker (2018) suggests that native-like second language acquisition can occur throughout the teen years. In addition, Vanhove (2013) and others have pointed out that most studies claiming early age advantages fail to account for factors other than age, such as the type and amount of exposure that older learners may have to the new language.

At any rate, having a realistic understanding of the value of "native-like" language competence is very important. For most communication, native-like language production is simply not necessary. Millions of individuals successfully communicate in nonnative languages that they have acquired to a high level of proficiency. And most languages have multiple dialects, meaning that there is a lot of diversity in accents even among "native speakers." For example, I am a native speaker of American English. But a highly proficient "nonnative English speaker" might have an accent that is more similar to mine than is a native speaker of Irish English. Given this diversity, even among "native speakers," there seems to be little advantage to advocating for "native-like" as a goal in language learning.

To summarize the question of age and second language acquisition: yes, children can probably more readily achieve native speaker-like production than can adults. However, recent research suggests that this ability might last throughout the teen years and not be limited to early childhood, as was previously thought.

Methodology

As we learned in chapter 2, when focusing on the second language acquisition of adults, 75 percent of language instruction should be devoted to *using* the language for meaningful communication and only 25 percent to learning abstract concepts *about* the language—discovering its grammar rules, word usage, etc. How do these percentages change in regard to the instruction of children?

Children at the early elementary level and younger don't benefit from grammar instruction. Again, grammar is an abstract concept, so young children aren't developmentally ready to understand it. The best approach to help young children acquire a new language is to use and use and use that language, at a level that is comprehensible to them.

By upper elementary and throughout the teen years (and beyond), two specific language teaching approaches are ideal for language acquisition:

- Content-based language teaching (CBLT): This approach utilizes the teaching of another content area, be it academic content, such as math or science, or other content, such as woodworking, sports, cooking, or a Bible study. This content is taught in the new language, and thus the new language is being acquired. For CBLT to be successful, teachers must gear the language of their instruction to the language level of the students. In other words, the teacher must ensure that the content and language are *comprehensible*.

- Task-based language teaching (TBLT): This approach focuses learners' attention on a task to be completed. For example, learners may need to produce a poster, write a letter, or interview someone. As students engage in the task, often in small groups, they use language necessary to complete the task, and thus are acquiring that language. (See my "English for Life" checklists in appendix B as an example of a task-based curriculum.)

CBLT and TBLT work very well together. Teachers can create tasks which explore specific content, planning for specific language use as students learn the content and engage in the task. These two approaches also work very well for adult learners, given a content and tasks that are meaningful to them.

Can it be helpful for children in upper elementary and above to have some targeted grammar and vocabulary instruction? Do they benefit from that 25 percent of language learning time? Some may, but many probably won't. For many children of all ages greater language gains will be made by focusing on real language use at their correct language level, rather than lessons about the language being learned. However, older children can benefit from attentive teachers who will know when jumping in with a brief grammatical explanation might be helpful.

Motivation

Motivation plays a significant role in second language acquisition. The adult language learner without sufficient motivation is unlikely to stay in the game over the long haul and reach high proficiency. Motivation is important for children as well, but it looks different at different stages.

Children in early elementary and younger are motivated by the here and now. Engaging classroom activities which provide enjoyable and interesting opportunities to use the language are what keep them motivated. Language teachers—and parents—sometimes err in talking to children about the eventual benefits of learning a new language. A much better strategy is just to make the day-to-day language acquisition experiences very interesting. This is why songs, chants, and games work so well with this age group.

Upper elementary children are typically motivated by discovery and accomplishment, making TBLT and CBLT great approaches for this age group. For example, in one of the English-learning textbooks that I wrote (*Passport to Adventure*, "Explore A"),[1] children work in small groups to create a water filtration system. As they read about water filtration, discuss in small groups, create poster illustrations, and present their projects, they are using their new language for real, meaningful, communicative purposes.

Middle school is an ideal time to focus on the *social* aspects of acquiring a new language (Taylor 2013). Developmentally, middle schoolers are motivated by social interaction, and this can be leveraged for language acquisition. Teachers and parents need to ensure that children at this age are engaged with empathetic peers who are helpful and supportive in the language acquisition process, and that children are able to hear and use language at their level of proficiency.

By high school, teens may be motivated by future work and study advantages, or ministry and service opportunities. They may be willing to put in the hard work of learning a language, through both *acquisition* and *learning* processes, for future reward or current opportunity. It is also true, though, that they may resist learning the language if they don't envision a future using the new language. For example, a high schooler moving with her family to Mozambique may see little advantage to learning Portuguese. If she is "biding her time" to return to the US for college and can't see how Portuguese would be advantageous to her in the future, then there is no future-oriented motivation. If we add a lack of involvement in current ministry or service, then there may also be no current motivation, and second language acquisition is not likely to occur.

Affective Factors

Affective factors play a tremendous role in second language acquisition at all ages. In other words, how a person feels about and amid their language learning is very important. As human beings, we are attracted to things that are enjoyable, interesting, and rewarding, and we tend to avoid things that are frustrating and stressful. The younger the person, the less willing they will be to endure frustration and stress for a greater long-term gain. How does this play out at various ages?

---

[1] *The Passport to Adventure, English as a Foreign Language Series for Children*, is produced by Purposeful Design, the publication arm of the Association of Christian Schools International (ACSI). More information is available here: https://www.acsi.org/textbooks/fca/esl.

It has been said that children love to learn … until they go to school! Unfortunately, mis-guided schooling has been responsible for a lot of stress and frustration in school, along with a general loss of the pure joy of learning. Successful second language acquisition programs for elementary-aged children will focus on using language through enjoyable experiences and activities. Ideally, young children don't receive grades on their language learning; instead they are simply assessed regularly to document what has been learned and what still needs to be learned, with instruction modified accordingly.

In middle school, stress factors to watch out for include unhealthy social situations. Situations in which a child doesn't feel supported and understood as she attempts to use a new language—or worse, is ridiculed and made fun of—can have a significant adverse effect on motivation. Though we, as parents, know that we can't shield our children from all difficult circumstances, we do want to vet situations very carefully for children moving into a new language and culture in adolescence. We need to be on the lookout for trauma that may occur in school, whether due to social situations, unrealistic academic expectations, or teachers who don't understand second language acquisition.

In the latter years of schooling, late teens are beginning to focus on their future, and stress levels may hinge on their perception of whether they are on track for the future they envision. If a child in grades 11 and 12 is doing well academically and social stresses are minimal, he may have the bandwidth to pursue opportunities to engage in language acquisition through friendships, family ministry, or service opportunities. However, he may also be more focused on his future back in his home country and see little reason to invest in learning a new language that he believes won't help him in the future.

Educational Options and Second Language Acquisition

Following this overview of various factors that affect second language acquisition for children of various ages, let's turn now to schooling options. Learning a language is not more important than getting an education, so parents must ensure that their children receive an effective education which will prepare them for their likely future. This should not be construed, however, as a promotion of so-called top-tier schools. Parents, as well as others, sometimes underestimate the potential for supposedly "poor" educational options to provide an adequate education.

To illustrate, I had a very checkered K-12 education, including a stint in a Brazilian school that was poor in every way: from resources to teacher knowledge and skill. (You can read about my story in greater detail in the excursus at the end of this chapter.) And yet I value those experiences today. I believe they did *not* prevent me from reaching my potential; in fact, I believe they have contributed to my success in my chosen field of language education.

When making choices about their children's education, parents of MKs have many factors to consider, in addition to overall educational quality. Identity, passport country, eventual repatriation, and college goals must be carefully considered as schooling options are chosen; and I will briefly reference these factors in the discussions of various schooling options below.

The primary purpose of this chapter, though, is to discuss language acquisition. Therefore we will look at the three main types of schooling used by missionary families today: English-medium schools, national (local language) schools, and homeschooling. We will consider the strengths and challenges of each, as pertaining to children's second language acquisition.

English-medium school

Many schools for MKs were started in the early days of the modern mission movement. Most of them were English-medium schools, and many of them remain in operation today. These schools often have a diverse student demographic—including, in addition to missionary families, expatriates in business and other sectors and local students. Many of these have held onto their Christian origin and are now called "International Christian Schools." I have experienced such schools from many different perspectives: as a student, parent, teacher, dorm parent, board chair, and consultant. These schools have facilitated missions by providing schooling for MKs and have contributed to the expansion of God's kingdom through excellence in teaching and curricula, which has produced men and women who are diligently carrying out the Great Commission in all corners of the globe.

However, the international Christian school movement has often failed in one key area: ensuring that students learn the local language. From Indonesia to Brazil to Germany to Tanzania … graduates of these schools, despite having attended the school five years or more, often did not learn the local language. Perhaps it has been assumed that the local language would be learned outside of school. This can happen, but often does not. School sometimes becomes all-consuming, leaving little time for outside interaction.

Fortunately, some international Christian schools are beginning to address this issue. A few schools, such as Black Forest Academy in Germany, now have bilingual programs helping foreign children to learn the local language and local children to learn English. Some are increasing the hours of instruction per week of their local language classes, as well as providing professional development for language teachers. Some are taking seriously the fact that their students are failing to engage in the local community, and therefore they are either building more community connections into the school curriculum or reducing school programming so that children have more time for engagement with the community outside of school.

An English-medium school may be the best educational choice as parents consider their children's eventual college goals and repatriation. However, parents should also investigate the school's level of commitment to language acquisition; and they can advocate for a strong local language program in the school. Such a program should include:

1. At least four hours of instruction weekly in the local language, preferably spread over four or five days.

2. Teachers who are trained in teaching a *second/foreign* language. This is not the same as having a degree in the language itself, or being trained to teach it to native speakers of that language. The school may be able to provide this training if trained teachers cannot be found.

3. Curricula and methodology that are developmentally appropriate and highly engaging. Students should be using the language for meaningful communication and engaging with the local community.

Parents need to keep in mind that school should only be one part of a child's life, not all of it. If the school dominates your family life, you can investigate the possibility of changing this dynamic. This will be explored more fully in the section called "Involvement in Ministry" below.

Though this book is primarily geared toward those whose native language is English, the focus of this chapter warrants some discussion for those whose family language is *not* English. If children don't speak English as their native language and are enrolled in an English-medium school, then there is more to consider regarding the acquisition of the local language. The first priority should always be to help children learn the school's language of instruction. Without the language of instruction, children are hindered in their ability to learn the academic content. So initially a child may need ESL (English as a Second Language) classes instead of classes in the local language. Ideally, ESL support should continue until a child has reached an intermediate level in English. How long this will take depends on both the child's age/grade and the level of English proficiency upon entering the school.

In most cases, until a child is able to navigate mainstream classes nearly as well as fully English-proficient peers, additional language learning time should be focused on learning English, not the local language. Also, for older children with low English proficiency, delayed participation in mainstream academic classes may be advised in order to provide the student time to learn foundational English, especially if an intensive, academic-language-focused English immersion program is available.

National school

Sending children to a local national school is not a new option, as evidenced by my own experience in Brazilian schools many years ago. But there has been increased focus on this educational option over the past twenty years or so (see Dormer 2009; Wrobbel 2008; and Wrobbel 2016). I want to clarify from the outset that this discussion about national schooling is geared to families who are expatriates in the country in which they are serving and to MKs who are not yet fluent in the local language. For families serving where one or both parents are not foreigners, or for children who have grown up bilingually and already speak the language used in local schools, the issues presented here may not apply.

As I have shared from my own story, my first Brazilian school experience was traumatic, because I spoke no Portuguese and no measures were taken by the school either to provide me with a means to communicate or to help me learn the language and the academic content.

Many years later, when my husband and I moved to Brazil with our daughters who were eight and nine, my childhood experience came vividly to mind, and I was fearful of putting my daughters into a Brazilian school. Still, there was no English-medium school where we lived, and I did want them to learn Portuguese. So a Brazilian school seemed like the best option. We found a school that would work with us, allowing us to tailor the girls' schedule and environment to their needs. Though they were a year apart in school, we initially put them in the same grade and brought in a tutor who would sit beside them in class and translate as needed. Flávia, a dynamic and fun-loving college student, sat beside them and helped them understand what was going on in the class. She took them out of the class when they needed a break, and taught them Portuguese through fun activities. Over time, Danna Jo and Jenna needed Flávia's help less and less. They learned Portuguese, succeeded in school, and love Flávia to this day!

Sometimes national school experiences go well. Children learn the language, make friends, and keep up with academics. Sometimes, however, schools are not flexible or supportive, children struggle academically because they can't understand, they can't make friends because they can't speak the language, and teachers don't know how to help them. Here are some issues to consider in deciding whether or not national schooling is a good option for your child.

The child's age

Generally speaking, the younger the child, the more likely national schooling can be a good fit. Young children use less language, academics are more hands-on and visual, and learning may be more engaging and experiential. If we add to this mix teachers who speak some English and can communicate with the child, and a willingness to differentiate instruction and assessment for a child who is not yet fluent in the local language, we may have a winner: a school environment in which a child can flourish both linguistically and academically.

Nevertheless, even at preschool level, the right school conditions are necessary in order for the experience to be a positive one. When we first moved to Indonesia, our youngest was four years old and we placed her in an Indonesian preschool. I'm glad I stayed with her every day at the school so that I could see what was happening. Though the teachers meant well, they spoke no English and therefore weren't able to communicate with Jenna. Also, the other children were a little fearful of her, likely because they had never interacted with a white child who didn't understand them. They didn't interact with her on the playground. My most vivid memory of that schooling experience is seeing Jenna up front with four Indonesian children during a presentation. There were two children on each side, standing as far away as possible from this tall, white, blond child in the middle. That solidified my decision to take Jenna out of that school! Mind you, the school, teacher, and other children weren't at fault. What happened was just what happens when kids can't communicate and the adults have no experience in facilitating communication across language barriers. Jenna was not learning much Indonesian, and leaving her in that situation would likely have resulted in negative feelings about the new language and culture.

As children progress in age, both language and content become more challenging. A child will likely struggle if placed in a situation where differentiation and direct language instruction are not provided. By mid-elementary and beyond, I wouldn't recommend putting a child into a school where there is no provision for helping the child understand what is going on. Even if the child has some basic understanding of the language, support in both academics and language learning are required.

The school's provisions and flexibility regarding language learners

In any school context in which a child isn't fully proficient in the language of instruction, the school should provide differentiated instruction for that child in order to ensure that he or she can both learn the language and understand the content. However, in many parts of the world schools receive very few children who don't speak the local language, and therefore they aren't prepared to help them. So the very first question to ask is, "*What kind of support and assistance do you provide for a child who is not fluent in the language of instruction?*" If the school indicates that they have a program to assist with language learning and teachers are trained to help students understand the academic content even while they are still learning the language, that is ideal, and the school may be a very good fit for your child. If you receive platitudes such as "Don't worry … children pick up languages easily!"—or worse, blank stares—those are indications that the school may not be a good fit.

Some schools may not have systems in place to accommodate foreign children, but may nevertheless welcome them and be very open to parent-initiated modifications and supports. Such was the case with the Brazilian school my children were in. Which modifications are needed depends on the age and grade of the child (the older the child, the more modifications will be needed), the child's personality and his/her own preferences, your own availability for support (for example, your ability to provide some schooling in your native language until the child is fully integrated into the school), and other cultural and logistical factors.

Here are some possible modifications for children learning the language of instruction:

- No academic grades given for the first year, or grades are based on effort or progress in the language, not on academic achievement.
- A daily pull-out time for instruction in the local language. You may need to provide the instructor for this. Ensure that the language instruction is developmentally appropriate, and focuses on real, meaningful, oral language use. Unfortunately, some teachers focus too much on grammar, spelling, literacy, etc., when oral language development is the first and most important need. If the school has mandatory English or other foreign language classes, this can be a good pull-out period for local language instruction.
- A tutor to sit by the child, at least until intermediate proficiency is reached. The tutor will translate or simplify oral and written language as needed, and provide encouragement and support for the child.
- Modified testing. Some modifications might include using a bilingual dictionary, having additional time, utilizing the tutor, and oral testing.
- Gradual integration into academic subjects, especially if a tutor in class is not used. Below is a typical order in which a child learning the language of instruction can effectively learn language and content in the various subjects. This list begins with those subjects that students could be placed in from the beginning because they are visual and not very language-dependent, ending with subjects that are very language-dense, in which students can probably only succeed after they have reached an intermediate level of language proficiency. Additional notes are also provided regarding the various subjects:

1. Physical Education
2. Art
3. Music
4. Math: This also depends on math aptitude and interest. If math is a struggle for the child, delay introduction to math in a foreign language and try to provide some grade-level math instruction in the native language.
5. Science: This also depends on the way science is taught. If it is very visual and experiential, and if the child finds it interesting, science could be introduced sooner.
6. Bible: If the child is in a Christian school that teaches Bible, and if the child is already familiar with many of the stories and concepts that are taught in the Bible class, this may be a good first "language-dense" subject for the child to be integrated into.
7. Social Studies: This is very language-dense and often requires considerable cultural background. Thus, it is often not advisable for children below intermediate-level proficiency.
8. Language Arts: The study of language by its own native speakers usually includes very advanced language, and an emphasis on grammar, reading, and writing, which is not very helpful for those learning the language as a second or foreign language. This is usually the best subject for the child to be pulled out of for language instruction.

Some schools may operate under very strict policies and norms which may preclude the implementation of some of the modifications suggested above. If that is the case, national schooling may not be the best option for your child until he or she has reached at least intermediate level proficiency in the local language.

Homeschool

With the surge in homeschooling in the 1980s (Gaither 2017), and the subsequent increase in resources and support for homeschooling families, came a shift in thinking about MK education. Far from the early days in missions when children were routinely sent off to boarding school, homeschooling has enabled families to stay together. Other advantages to homeschooling include flexibility in location, as homeschooling families don't need to be located near good schools, and the considerable cost savings over private schooling. Increasingly, as well, online distance education options are available. Families might be able to utilize online educational options to supplement a homeschooling curriculum in subjects in which the parents lack expertise or resources. Or a child might be enrolled in a full-service online school that provides real-time, video-based instruction in all subjects. Our daughters were enrolled in such a school, based in the US, for their middle school years. They started in this online school while we lived in Brazil, as we had decided to switch from Brazilian schooling to an English curriculum when they reached middle school age. They remained in this school while we were on a six-month furlough in Canada, which provided consistency and made it possible for us to travel as a family for speaking engagements. In short, homeschooling, especially now with emerging internet schooling options, may have numerous advantages.

Still, homeschooling on the mission field can present challenges. First, it is likely a full-time job for one parent. Though the amount of time required is impacted by the number of children and the type of homeschooling, it frequently takes more time and energy than parents think it will. It is either one parent's full-time ministry or both parents' part-time ministry.

Second, resources, support, and homeschool groups that would be accessible to homeschooling families in the home country may not be available overseas.

Finally, though the flexibility of homeschooling should provide opportunities for community engagement and thus language and culture learning, some mission agencies are reporting that homeschooling families are the least engaged in local communities. The teaching parent, often the mother, may not attend language school and thus struggle herself to learn the local language. Community connections that would be made by having children in a local school aren't made, and homeschooling can become an easy excuse for not getting out of the house, talking to the neighbors, and learning the language. These dynamics can have a negative impact on the family's ministry and longevity of service.

With forethought and planning, however, these challenges can be overcome; and homeschooling can be an excellent option for some missionary families, especially those who don't have other good schooling options. In fact, I believe the flexibility inherent in homeschooling can be leveraged for excellent language and culture learning by all family members.

The first step is to prioritize language and culture learning. It can be easy to fall into the trap of seeing grade-level academic curriculum as urgent. But it's usually not. There is usually no downside, for example, to skipping the fourth-grade social studies and health curricula and using that time instead for language and culture learning. Even less mandatory is the sequencing of high school subjects. All subjects aren't needed every year; and, in fact, it often makes good educational sense to focus on one subject at a time. So it might be very possible to pare down academic subjects for the first semester in the new country, in favor of an intensive focus on learning the local language and culture. A local language tutor might be able to come into the home and provide language instruction for the whole family. At beginning language levels, adults and children can often benefit from the same instructional methods—songs, games, and lots of meaningful and engaging communication—and language acquisition can be an excellent family activity. If a tutor can come into the home for two to three hours a day for the first few months, a basic foundation in the new language can be achieved.

An equally important goal is to integrate into the local community. A language acquisition curriculum which poses tasks requiring interaction with individuals outside of the home can be very helpful. For example, after learning family words, a task might be to have a conversation with someone from the community, telling them about the family. Ensure that there is adequate preparation with the language tutor first, as indicated in chapter 3. But the point is that homeschooling can provide the kind of flexibility which makes such interactions not only possible, but in fact an integral part of the homeschooling curriculum.

None of this happens, though, without a strong commitment on the part of both the parents and the mission agency to prioritizing language acquisition for the first six to twelve months in the country. Where the accountability of a formal school isn't present, a great deal of discipline and perseverance are required to pursue language learning and community engagement. It may work well to design a plan and then identify someone who can provide accountability for sticking to the plan.

Preparing children for language learning

No matter what schooling option is chosen, and no matter how the local language will be acquired, children need a voice in the conversation. Children as young as early elementary can understand various schooling options and engage in fruitful discussions about learning a new language. In my experience, most MKs initially want to learn the language and will benefit from having a voice in how that happens. However, if language learning experiences are negative or ineffective, that initial willingness can quickly turn into a distaste for language learning—and even bitterness about being on the mission field. This is why it is so very important to ensure that children experience good age appropriate and language level appropriate methodologies, in programs in which they have a voice and are heard.

Involvement in Ministry

Children in any location benefit from involvement in ministry and service to others. On the mission field, participation in their parents' ministry is often a natural fit for MKs. Growing up, I helped teach Sunday school, worked alongside my mom doing laundry for visiting work teams, and sang with my brothers in churches. Our own daughters did much the same, helping in English camps and contributing in many ways to our ministry in Indonesia and Brazil.

That said, like anything, this perspective can be taken to the extreme. An adult MK friend of mine still has an edge of bitterness in his voice as he recalls being forced to hand out tracts at train stations on Christmas day. This isn't the kind of family ministry engagement I'm talking about. Rather, it's involvement that is voluntary (or at least mostly so!) and sensitive to the feelings and needs of all family members, and which has the ability not only to bless others with service, but to strengthen family bonds.

For example, during our second term in Indonesia our daughter, then in high school, developed an interest in community health issues. For a time, Jenna was able to assist a colleague of ours in her physical therapy ministry, which was very rewarding for her. Had I insisted that Jenna continue to help me in English teaching rather than giving her the opportunity to choose where she wanted to be involved, she wouldn't have learned about another area of ministry, and our family life may have been negatively impacted.

Though children may be able to engage in some type of ministry without knowing the local language, those options are usually limited. Ministry within the new culture will often be limited if children don't learn the local language. Therefore, no matter which educational option is chosen, it is worth engaging in discussion as a family and with mission leaders about how, exactly, the language will be acquired by *all* members of the family.

Sometimes ministry and language-learning opportunities can go hand in hand. For example, an older child might provide babysitting services for a local child and learn some basic language from the child. Or a neighbor might request help with English, and an agreement could be made to have two-way language learning sessions. Or perhaps an older child can play the guitar or piano for a local worship band, and thus be learning songs in the local language. There are many ways in which a service or ministry opportunity could also provide input in the local language. If families engage in regular dialogue, prioritizing ministry, language learning, and the well-being of each family member, you might be surprised at the creative ways God can meet language learning needs.

Charting the Best Course

To recap, here are the essential goals for families and mission agencies to keep in mind as they make critical decisions about education and language acquisition:

1. Children's emotional, physical, and spiritual well-being is paramount. This doesn't mean that we need to envision a stress-free path for our children or shield them from difficulties. In fact, one of the best things parents can do is to walk alongside their children as they encounter developmentally appropriate challenges, providing the resources and support to meet these challenges. However, this does mean considering carefully the long-term effects of our choices.

2. Children need appropriate K-12 schooling which will prepare them for college and career, and probably also repatriation. Again, this need not be perfect schooling, and sometimes short periods in a difficult school situation can bring long-term good. Such was the case with my few months in a poor Brazilian school, which solidified my Portuguese and didn't harm me in the long run. Most parents, however, do envision that their children will eventually repatriate back to their passport country for college and adult life. This fact needs to be taken into consideration in the choice of schooling. For us, that meant switching our Canadian-American daughters from Portuguese to English medium education in middle school.

3. Children need good opportunities to learn the local language. It is much more difficult for children to integrate into the local culture, and to appreciate their new home, if they don't speak the language. It can also have a fracturing effect on the family, resulting in situations such as the father going to a local church for ministry while the rest of the family attends an English-speaking church. Children don't just pick up languages effortlessly, and conscious planning is required to ensure that children have good opportunities to learn the language.

4. Families benefit from engaging in ministry together. Parents, of course, will be engaged in a lot of ministry beyond that which might be appropriate for the family. However, finding some ministry opportunities that children can participate in is a very good thing. Make sure that these are developmentally appropriate, that children have a voice in their activities, and that all family needs and realities are considered.

Can Children Lose Their First Language?

There seems to be enough anecdotal evidence as well as research findings to suggest that this can indeed happen. If a young child is suddenly immersed in a new language environment, as may happen, for example, at school or through international adoption, and the first language is not maintained at home, the quick language acquisition that appears to take place may actually be a language replacement rather than a language addition (Bialystok and Hakuta 1994).

A more common difficulty experienced by families in cross-cultural ministry is the lack of *active* development of the first language. If a child's only exposure to their native language is in their home, he or she will likely not develop an academic level of that language without concerted effort on the part of the parents.

When our daughters were in Brazilian school, we began noticing their lack of English words when talking about their studies. So each evening we built in a short time of "school talk" in our home. We asked the girls to tell us what they were learning. If they shared using Portuguese words, we would supply the

English terms and then have them re-state what they had shared, using English. This worked well at the elementary school level.... I'm not sure we would have been able to supply the correct English terms when they reached high school! By conscientiously focusing on their academic English development, Danna Jo and Jenna were able to successfully transition to English-medium online education after three years in Brazilian school.

One caution here: I think our daughters willingly participated in this because it was family time and we made it fun. This isn't the same as sending children to after-school or Saturday programs in their native language. These efforts are often minimally effective because the children don't get enough down time and because the content of these programs is not connected to what the children are learning in school.

Raising Children Bilingually

The final segment of this chapter is for those parents who have the desire and means to raise children bilingually. *Simultaneous bilingualism* is the term sometimes used to describe the development of two first, or native, languages. This is contrasted with *sequential bilingualism*, in which an additional language is acquired after age four or five, when the native language has been internalized well. Bilingualism has been linked to higher cognitive abilities and provides increased opportunities in work and study. So raising a child bilingually has no real downside. However, it is good to understand what is involved in raising a child bilingually, and how to make the experience positive. Understanding the issues addressed below can lessen parents' concerns and help the family to fully embrace the bilingual home experience.

Do bilingual children experience language delays?
Bilingual infants and toddlers have double the language acquisition task, so it isn't unusual for their language development to be delayed in comparison to monolingual children in either of the languages. In the early school years, bilingual children may seem to have smaller vocabularies than their monolingual counterparts. However, if words from *both* languages are counted, the vocabulary of bilinguals is usually considerably higher. Be encouraged by the fact that any delays, compared to that of monolinguals, are short-lived. In the long run, usually at least by late elementary, bilinguals catch up to and often surpass their monolingual peers in language development.

How should the languages be separated?
A child must regularly interact with individuals in both languages for simultaneous bilingualism to occur. Oftentimes, each parent has a different native language

and uses this language consistently with the child. Or perhaps a caregiver, such as a nanny, grandparent, or neighbor, spends considerable time with the child, interacting with the child in a language different than that of the parents. It is widely thought that the best way to "divide" the languages is for each individual to speak consistently in only one language. This may be a way to ensure that the child receives roughly equivalent input in each language; and each parent or caregiver speaking in his/her native language ensures that the child is receiving quality language input.

This is certainly not the only way to raise a child bilingually, however. For example, if both parents are proficient in both languages, they can each use both languages with the child. Most important, according to Fred Genesee, a well-known author on the topic of childhood bilingualism, is that children receive "continuous, sustained, and enriched exposure to both languages" (Genesee 2007, 8).

How much input in a language is necessary?
Children may be at risk of not developing full competence in one of their languages if they don't receive sufficient input, as Genesee explains:

> It is clear that children learning two languages at the same time do not need as much exposure to each language as monolingual children get for their one. However, there is a minimum level of exposure below which the development of that language can be delayed and incomplete. We do not have solid scientific evidence to tell us what that minimum amount of exposure is. Our best guess at this time is that bilingual children must be exposed to a language during at least 30% of their total language exposure if their acquisition of that language is to proceed normally. Less exposure than this could result in incomplete acquisition of that language. (2007, 6)

Is "code-switching" a problem?
When bilinguals speak, they may switch between languages—often called "code-switching." There are many perfectly good reasons for this. Since bilinguals rarely know all the same words in each language, code switching allows them to express meaning more precisely. Sometimes switching between languages is intentional and purposeful and is done for specific communicative and social reasons. This practice, which has recently become known as "translanguaging," is viewed positively, as an expression of linguistic skill rather than deficit (see, for example, Creese and Blackledge 2010; and García and Wei 2013). Many studies are currently underway about the nature of translanguaging and its impact on the development of bi- and multi-lingualism. Until we have more conclusive evidence, parents can rest assured that code-switching (or, "translanguaging" is normal and not considered detrimental. However, Genesee's guidance here

remains prudent: "As long as most people in the child's family and community use only one language at a time, the child will learn that this is the appropriate way to use their two languages" (2007, 6).

Conclusion

Until recently, too little attention has been given to the language development of MKs. Though mission organizations have made strides in addressing the overall educational needs of MKs and providing better direction to parents as they choose from among various educational options, it's still not common that preparation for missionary service includes a realistic discussion of how the children will learn the local language. Mission leaders and missionary candidates alike need to realize that children need an optimal environment for learning a new language, just as their parents do. Without a conscious focus on the language acquisition of the children, the parents may find their envisioned ministry to be short-circuited and their family life and ministry to be fragmented.

Jan's Brazilian School Experiences
An Excursus on My Brazilian School Experiences

My education was unconventional to say the least. I began school in rural Indiana and graduated in a class of one in Londrina, Brazil, through a correspondence course. What transpired in between was twelve different schools and all types of schooling: from American public school, to national Brazilian Christian and public schools, to boarding school, to Christian international school, and finally to distance education. Such a school life could only have been orchestrated by God, in order to provide me with rewarding and challenging experiences that would equip me for the educational roles God has placed me in today. Here I want to share specifically about my two Brazilian school experiences, because I believe that these had a significant impact on my life and vocation.

While my parents were in language school, they decided to place my brother, age twelve, and me, age ten, in a private Christian Brazilian school so that we could learn Portuguese. Back in 1970, people generally believed that children just "soak up" a new language; and a prevailing thought in missions was to immerse kids in a local national school where they supposedly would learn the language quickly. I'm sure I embraced this decision at the time, since I had been excited about moving to Brazil and was eager to learn Portuguese.

Then came the first day of school. I remember it well. Arriving at the school, I stood in the courtyard in my cute little navy skirt, white blouse, and red belt, the school uniform which I had proudly donned that morning … and was engulfed in fear. For the first time, I could understand nothing around me. I had been hearing Portuguese, of course, since our arrival, but now I was all alone, hearing *no* English at all. Some girls yelled something at me—but I didn't know if they were asking me to join them or telling me to get lost. I knew my brother was somewhere on the school grounds, but I didn't know where. Our recess times were different, and I never saw him.

The classroom was even worse than the courtyard. The teacher yelled, and I thought she was yelling at me. (I discovered later that this was simply a typical teaching style in Brazilian schools at that time, and the raised voice was not targeting me specifically.) The teacher must not have known any English, because she never spoke a word of English to me. I had been a good student in American school, and I loved to learn. But here I saw strange words on the board and on worksheets. Even the handwriting was different, and I struggled to make out some of the letters. I didn't know what to do. I tried to copy some of the words in my notebook, but didn't know what I was writing down.

Another American missionary kid, a boy, joined my class at some point. But the teacher didn't want us to speak in English to each other. Also, he got in trouble a lot, and that's the last thing I wanted to do!

I cried many nights. For a while, my parents didn't know this. And my teacher never knew. I'm sure she thought I was learning something and was fine. But I wasn't fine, and thanks to parents who cared more about their little girl than about was what considered the "best" thing to do to help children learn language, they soon took us out of that school. There was nothing wrong with the school or the teachers; it's just not possible to grow and learn as a fourth-grader should when you have no means of communication.

Then my parents hired a Brazilian tutor to come to our home to help us kids learn Portuguese. And I made a happy discovery: I loved learning Portuguese! Now things made sense! The tutor would draw pictures and write the words. We got to practice simple phrases: *Bom dia! Tudo bem? Tudo bem!* I felt successful in Portuguese for the first time since coming to Brazil.

When my parents were finished with language school, we moved to interior Brazil, where my parents would be developing a youth camp. The plan was to homeschool. But my mom was expecting another child by then, and the challenges of life in the interior, with few amenities, meant that there was little time for homeschooling, plus difficulty even getting school materials. So we began to look at the local public school as perhaps the best solution for me, now in fifth grade. I was anxious to try Brazilian school again, because by this time I could communicate some in Portuguese.

The poor public school in interior Brazil was a far cry from the private Christian school we had attended earlier. Our "school bus" was a dump truck. Apparently this was the only vehicle the town could find to pick up the "country" kids and bring us into town for school. The dump truck couldn't be spared to bring us home after school, though. So a Brazilian friend, Clarice, and I walked the five miles home. Sometimes we were able to catch rides on horse carts or tractors. But other days, we played a rock-throwing and skipping game, to pass the time, all the way home. The time I spent with Clarice during our school days is one of my cherished memories of growing up in Brazil.

There were about forty kids in my class, and we sat two to a bench at rough wooden tables upon which decades of students before us had done their work. There was nothing on the walls and nothing but a rough chalkboard at the front of the room. We didn't have textbooks or worksheets. We had notebooks for each subject, and school consisted of the subject teachers coming in with their textbook, writing the text on the board, and telling us to copy it in our notebooks.

There was no real "teaching" that I can recall. Fortunately, I excelled in copying and memorizing for tests, so I did well. And I did learn some things. To this day I can sing all the stanzas of the Brazilian national anthem, and I can still see in my mind's eye my beautiful colored maps drawn into my geography notebook.

My two Brazilian school experiences no doubt helped to lead me into the profession of language education that I love today. I regularly train teachers to meet the needs of English learners in schools. Every time I speak with teachers, I remember being that frightened fourth-grade girl who just needed a chance to learn some Portuguese before being immersed in Brazilian school. I also share about being in a poor school that had nothing, but in which I actually learned, because I had the crucial skill needed for learning: language.

As I look back on my educational life, I see God's hand at work. He never let me go, and he has used all the twists and turns in my educational narrative for his good in preparing me for his service.

Opportunities for Ministry amid Language Learning

AARON

We've just been here a couple of months, but I feel like the passion that brought me here is all but gone. I go to language classes and just sit there learning words and grammar rules. And frankly, I just feel so useless. I was so involved in ministry back home: Bible studies, counseling, mentoring—I loved it all. You know ... connecting with people. But this—this day in, day out, focus just on language and not people—is killing me. I'm not sure I can take another six months of this.

If you are already in your place of service, perhaps Aaron's frustration resonates with you. Especially if you had an active ministry "back home," the language learning period can seem like an endless desert stretching out before you—a time when you are "on hold," waiting for a future, elusive ministry.

I don't think it needs to be like this, and my perspective of language learning time as ministry comes from several realities. First, good language acquisition experiences involve *people*. If you are stuck in a program where you are not interacting with people, something needs to change! Where there are people, there are always opportunities for ministry. Second, the language learning period provides some unique opportunities that a person who speaks the local language well may not have. Authentic needs—in essence, your neediness as a language learner—can be the very impetus for interaction that can be just as ministry oriented as later endeavors might be. And finally, we now know the negative role that stress plays in hindering language acquisition. If engaging in some kind of ministry, even through your native language, reduces your level of stress by allowing you to maintain a sense of your former identity, then it may contribute to your overall well-being and therefore to your long-term language learning success.

Ministry through Language Learning: Rod's Experience

It was early 1999, and Rod and I, along with our two daughters, ages eight and nine, had just arrived in Brazil. Having grown up in Brazil, I spoke Portuguese well. But Rod and our daughters faced the arduous task of learning a language in which some verbs can have over one hundred different endings! We placed Danna Jo and Jenna in Brazilian school, as I shared in the previous chapter, and Rod, a self-declared "poor language learner," started plugging away in language lessons.

Our first assignment in Brazil was to run a youth camp for a year, while the missionary couple that had been running the camp went on home assignment. The mission had been unable to find someone to fill in at the camp, and because I spoke the language and had lived in the area as a child, and because of Rod's years of experience in youth ministry, we were able to step into this role for a year. But Rod needed an assistant during the youth camps, someone who could speak some English and also participate in—and learn—youth ministry.

Enter Diogo. Having come to know the Lord as a result of the ministry of my brother and sister-in-law, Jay and Kirsten, in central Brazil, Diogo had felt the call to ministry and was now enrolled in our seminary near the camp. He also had learned some English from Jay and Kirsten, and was eager to improve his English during his time in seminary. It was a perfect partnership. Rod needed someone by his side who could not only translate but help him learn Portuguese. Diogo wanted someone to interact with in English and to help him learn about ministry. Both men got what they needed; and as Rod learned more Portuguese, the relationship eventually morphed into mentorship more than language learning. Rod had the opportunity to mentor Diogo throughout his time in seminary, and then during his first church placement. Diogo went on to plant two churches and pursue advanced pastoral studies, and today he credits much of his ministry formation to Rod's mentorship. This relationship would likely never have developed were it not for Rod's need to learn Portuguese and his need for help in ministry as he learned. Rod's language needs provided the context and rationale for hours spent working with a young man eager for mentorship.

In this chapter I will address five ways in which the language learning phase of cross-cultural service may provide opportunities for ministry: 1) Establishing relationships with those who provide language assistance, as we have seen in the case of Rod and Diogo; 2) Developing and demonstrating the posture of a humble learner; 3) Teaching English; 4) Acting as a Christian witness in a secular language program; and 5) Providing opportunities for local residents to see their culture and practices through a new lens.

Establishing Relationships with Those Providing Language Assistance

The vulnerability experienced while learning a new language provides the perfect foundation for relationship-building. Any thought that locals may have about outsiders coming in with superior knowledge and education tends to diminish as they hear the foreigner struggling to put together a sentence that a native three-year-old can utter fluently. Rod's lack of Portuguese, and the fact that Diogo's English, while still developing, was significantly higher than Rod's Portuguese, created a level playing field for interaction. Rod had many more years of life and ministry experience. But as a newbie in Portuguese and in Brazilian culture, he needed Diogo's help.

Planned and purposeful "language helper" relationships can lead to life-impacting ministry. In many areas of the world, there are people with sufficient English language skills to serve as language helpers. In some situations, this may be a relationship between friends, with the agreement that local language assistance is offered in exchange for the opportunity to practice English, as was the case for Diogo and Rod. Or it might be appropriate to pay the language helper, providing meaningful work in a setting where jobs are scarce. Whether or not there is a financial arrangement, planning and purpose are central to the goals of developing a mentoring relationship with a language helper. Think through these questions prior to entering into an arrangement:

1. Would the language helper genuinely appreciate the relationship, and benefit from both providing and receiving assistance?

2. Do the personalities and time availability of each person lend themselves more to formality or informality? Rod and Diogo had an informal relationship, with no specific language or mentoring goals in mind. In some contexts, however, it is possible to have more formal planning in regard to both mentoring and language learning. Where planning language goals is concerned, the tips provided on page 52 in chapter 4 can be used to guide sessions with a language helper.

3. Is compensation appropriate, expected, and/or needed, given the local culture and the situation of the language helper?

Of course, the cross-cultural worker just arriving in the country may not be in a position to answer these questions or find a language helper. This may need to be done by those who are already in the country and have a network of contacts.

Developing and Demonstrating the Posture of a Humble Learner

During the first few years in a new country, language learning and culture learning is cross-cultural workers' main focus. We are authentically and transparently new to the country, culture, and language, needing the help of locals as we seek to understand and integrate into our new community. We don't know how greetings occur, how friends console one another in difficult times, or what is celebrated and how. We may not understand the meanings of holidays or the positioning of religious views and practices within the culture. On a more basic level, we may not even know where to buy food or how to fix it. And so as we begin our tenure in a new language and culture, it is likely quite obvious to everyone that we are learners.

Though this may be a time of frustration as we feel lost in a new cultural environment and must rely on and learn from others, the humility that we can develop and demonstrate during this period provides the best possible foundation for all of our future ministry. Don Snow (2001) claims that it is only as we come into a culture understanding our position as learners that we can demonstrate the humility which must preface all our interactions in that new culture.

Jesus' words, "Blessed are the meek," never meant so much to me as when we moved to Indonesia and I found myself totally out of my element in a culture unlike any I had previously experienced. I felt lost and humbled by my inability to find my own way in a new environment. Having always prided myself on self-sufficiency, I was now at the mercy of neighbors for simple and basic needs, such as getting a horse-cart ride to town or knowing when the road would be blocked off for a celebration.

Many individuals who move to a new country recount similar stories and feelings. After the first few years in a new country, however, we have typically learned a great deal about our new home and feel more self-sufficient. Unfortunately, this can result in a loss of that initial "learner" positioning that is so vital throughout our ministry. So the initial language learning phase presents us with a unique opportunity to develop a posture of humility as we genuinely reach out to engage with and learn from others. As we do, we can notice and reflect on the perspectives we are developing so that we can strive to consciously maintain them even when we begin to feel more at home and more confident in our abilities to navigate the new language and culture.

Teaching English

This one might surprise you. How can teaching English help you as you begin to learn a new language? Language learning is enhanced as a person develops linguistic awareness. That is, the more aware you are of how languages work, the greater your ability to understand various features of your new language. Linguistic awareness is not only developed as you study a *new* language; learning more about your native language helps too. In fact, successful language learners work to understand how their own language functions in order to be able to compare and contrast it with their new language. And if you are a native English speaker, what better way to learn more about your native language than to teach it to someone else? I certainly agree with the adage that the highest form of learning comes through teaching. Accordingly, teaching English can help grow your linguistic awareness and make you a better language learner.

Teaching English can also provide a means for developing initial relationships in a new environment. As you get to know a school, a class, or even just an individual in a tutoring arrangement, you begin building a network of acquaintances in a new place. Depending on your time availability for teaching English, additional opportunities can take place, such as practicing English over coffee or having a community English movie night. Many ministry networks have begun because someone wanted help with English, and an English-speaking cross-cultural worker was willing to see it as an opportunity to build a relationship.

Another possible benefit of teaching English is simply being able to engage in some kind of service to others as you are learning the local language. It can help restore your sense of self to be able to spend a little time ministering in your native language. It can help provide some balance during a period of time that can be stressful and overwhelming. Since many people in most parts of the world would greatly appreciate having someone help them with English, why not use this time before you are able to minister through the local language to minister through English? It can be a blessing for English-learners and for you.

There are a couple of caveats regarding teaching English in your new culture, however. No one should teach English without *some* training in teaching English. I address this issue at length in my book *Teaching English in Missions: Effectiveness and Integrity* (Dormer 2011). In the opening chapter, I pose this question: If you can speak English, you can teach it: true or false? As the chapter unfolds, telling the story of "Bill" floundering as he attempted to teach an English class for which he was unprepared, the answer is clear: The ability to speak English is *not* sufficient preparation for teaching it!

But, you might argue, if English teaching is not to be your long-term ministry, why invest time and money in a course to help you understand the teaching of English? Again, understanding your own language from a linguistic perspective is quite helpful in your effort to acquire a new language. And in a TESOL (Teaching English to Speakers of Other Languages) preparation course, you won't get just the linguistic background. You will also learn how languages are acquired, and this learning can assist you tremendously in your efforts to learn a new language. In addition, cross-cultural workers who never expected to teach English often *do* find themselves in that position. I think it's hard to see how a short preservice course in teaching English could be anything but valuable in preparing for cross-cultural ministry.

The second caveat pertains to time and priority. It is possible to become so immersed in teaching English that no time is left for your *own* language learning. And make no mistake: Learning your new language must still be your priority! The ability to initiate ministry through teaching English is great. It can help you as you learn your new language and culture, and it can provide you with a way to connect with people that isn't dependent on proficiency in the new language. But learning the local language well is still vital for your long-term ministry, and should not be sidelined.

Acting as a Christian Witness in a Secular Language Program

One thing I love about the field of language teaching is that it is so learner centered. Good language teaching *always* begins with the question, "What language does the learner need?" and uses this needs analysis as a basis for designing the curriculum and selecting the materials. For example, if I, as a Christian English teacher, have a Muslim student in my class who desires to be able to explain the practice of Ramadan in English, I should provide English lessons for that student which will enable him or her to meet that goal. If I was unfamiliar with Islam, I would need to learn about the religion and the fasting month of Ramadan in order to provide my student with appropriate language to explain it in English.

If I was a cross-cultural worker enrolled in a secular language program and I would like to learn the language of the Bible, religion, beliefs, and values in the local language, the teacher should honor my desire in the framing of the class. A good language teacher, regardless of his or her values or beliefs, would seek to meet a student's language learning needs by incorporating the Bible, topics of religion, discussions about values, and other similar components into the language lessons. Of course, context is everything. There may be situations in which it isn't appropriate to request the study of the Bible or Christian topics. But in many places this would be permissible and a language teacher might appreciate learning about the Christian faith.

Understanding this "best practice" in language teaching might cause us to think a bit differently about our selection of language school experiences. Is it really best to use language schools created just for missionaries? This kind of environment is comfortable, of course, but might secular learning contexts provide more contact with the "real world" within the new country? Might it provide missionaries with opportunities for Christian witness, while they are also learning about the local educational and cultural context?

The answer to these questions, of course, depends on many factors in regard to the culture, the language learning options, and most of all, the individual or family learning the language. And while enrolling in a secular course in part to be a Christian witness may be a good path to consider, we should also ensure that our perspective remains that of a learner in a new culture. Even though it's legitimate to ask to learn language pertaining to the Bible and Christianity, such an approach should be tempered with love and respect for teachers who are not Christians. Language learners in a secular environment should still seek to *learn* rather than proselytize, *suggest* rather than insist, and *respect* rather than force. Nevertheless, if all this is taken into consideration and the posture of a humble learner within the new culture is well maintained, language study within a secular environment can provide fruitful opportunities for Christian witness.

Providing Opportunities for Local Residents to See Their Culture and Practices through a New Lens

The last opportunity for ministry during the initial language learning years that I will mention involves the fact that foreigners bring a different set of eyes to the local environment. This reality is sometimes framed as a drawback. Imagine, for example, a context in which it is customary for everyone in the family to help themselves to food at any time and never eat together as a family. We may conclude that this practice hinders the development of family relationships. Our perspective no doubt fails to understand many circumstances resulting in this practice, such as family members coming and going at different times for work and study, or even perhaps that there aren't enough dishes or chairs for everyone to sit and eat at the same time. We would certainly be in error if we were to quickly draw a negative generalization about the culture based on the fact that families don't eat together. We should, instead, reserve judgment and seek to understand the situation more fully.

On the other hand, though, our desire to understand the realities more fully can result in rich conversations with locals (provided that either their English or our emerging local language is sufficient for the task) as we seek to understand. As outsiders, we may have opportunities to ask questions that others cannot ask. As we ask questions, questions are often asked back about our own traditions. As we share about our own culture and perspectives, locals have an opportunity to see their traditions through a new lens.

All cultures are a combination of strengths and weaknesses. As we are immersed in a new culture as *learners*, we can more easily see our own culture through a new lens, perhaps identifying cultural habits or traditions that we want to change or modify in our own families. And sometimes there are things in our new location which would benefit from a view through a different lens as well, and our positioning as newcomers in the culture can afford us the opportunity to ask questions, and thus share a new perspective. (For more on this topic, see *The Gift of the Stranger*, by Smith and Carvill 2000.)

Beth, a short-termer, came to Brazil to learn Portuguese before heading to Mozambique. In one of her Portuguese classes she was assigned to learn about Brazilian culture regarding mealtimes. So Beth asked Luciana, a college student who was her Brazilian language partner, many questions, such as what was typically eaten for breakfast and when families sat down for meals and conversation together. Luciana seemed surprised at this question, and said that her family never had meals together at home—but only in restaurants. After nodding in understanding, Beth proceeded to jot down the response in her conversation journal. But Luciana asked, "Do Americans do that? Sit down and eat together every night? I see that in the movies, but I thought it was just in the movies."

Beth replied that families have different traditions, but in her family dinnertime together, accompanied by sharing about the day, was highly valued. That conversation had a significant impact on Luciana, as she was able to view "dinnertime" through a different lens. She was able to catch a glimpse of a different picture of family life. In fact, she told me later that because of her interactions with Beth she had determined that when she had a family of her own, they were going to eat and share together every day, and "not be strangers."

Conclusion

I often hear conversations among missionary personnel about the dangers of getting into ministry before the language has been learned. But I have seen rich, ministry-driven relationships emerge *because* the foreigner was new to the language and culture, not in spite of it. The language acquisition phase in the life of a cross-cultural worker is hard enough without also putting limits on those elements that might bring satisfaction and reward during this difficult phase. With proper positioning as a humble learner, with adequate training—for example, in second language acquisition and TESOL—and finally, with good planning that balances language acquisition time with emerging ministry engagement, the language learning phase does not have to be an emotional or ministerial desert.

Applying New Understanding to Chart a Path for Success

MANDY

I get it now. There's a lot more to know about language learning than I thought there was! I'm really happy about what I've learned in this book, but now I'm afraid I won't be able to remember it all. How can I make sure I really do consider the right things when I make choices about my language studies? What if I get on the field and forget everything, and I'm too busy to reread the parts I need to remember?

At this point, you may be feeling like Mandy. This book has provided a lot of information. If you had not read or heard much about language acquisition previously, then much of this information was probably new, and maybe a little overwhelming. This final chapter will provide a review, as well as some tools that may help you apply (and remember!) some of what you learned.

But first, let's revisit your initial perspectives recorded in chapter 1. Return to the survey on page 2. Read through your initial thoughts there, noting what ideas, beliefs and assumptions may have changed. Then, read my brief summaries below regarding each of the statements in the survey.

Revisiting the Initial Survey

1. **Children are better language learners than adults.**
   Not really. Children will more easily acquire native-like language in areas such as pronunciation, but native-like speech is overrated. Older learners can learn more new words and structures in the same amount of time, given good conditions, and this results in greater language learning overall.

2. **Children have fewer inhibitions than adults about using new language.**
   "Inhibition" is a characteristic of personality and environment, not age. Adults may be more willing to get past their inhibitions because they can be more intentional in achieving their goals.

3. **Children can hear and reproduce new sounds better than adults.**
   This is true. Children can probably achieve more native-like pronunciation than adults, and we now know that this ability to achieve native-like competence extends through the teen years, and probably does not end in early childhood or puberty, as has been suggested.

4. **There is a "critical age" above which it is more difficult to learn a language.**
   There is no proven "critical period" for second language acquisition. Throughout adulthood people can learn new languages, though in late adulthood it may be harder to engage in any kind of new learning, including learning languages.

5. **Language aptitude tests are good at predicting language learning success.**
   Most language aptitude tests focus on identifying language structures and patterns and on hearing sounds. This reduces language to a very narrow set of skills and ignores many other abilities and behaviors, such as a willingness to communicate, which may also predict language learning success.

6. **Success in language learning is measured by the ability to communicate.**
   Yes. Any measure of "success" in learning a new language should focus on the ability to authentically communicate with people in that language.

7. **Some people can't learn new languages.**
   Given good learning conditions and sufficient time, most people can learn a new language.

8. **Language learning is quick and easy for some people.**
   Learning a new language takes many, many hours, over many months, even for those who seem to learn "quickly." Individuals who enjoy the language learning experience may spend more time in language learning tasks, and therefore seem to make faster progress.

9. **The more you are immersed in a new language, the faster you will learn.**
   It is important to have sufficient language input at the right level. But while we do need a lot of input to learn a language, we also need breaks and pacing. Additional language immersion after reaching points of saturation is not usually helpful.
10. **We learn language in a predictable sequence.**
    Broadly speaking, yes—language is learned in a predictable sequence, with easier words and structures learned before more difficult ones. This doesn't mean, however, that an exact sequence of items to learn is best.
11. **It's not important to understand how the language works; we just need to use it.** While most of language acquisition does hinge on language use, adult language learners usually also benefit from understanding language structures. Good language lessons might involve 75 percent using the language, and 25 percent learning about the language.
12. **It takes one to two years to learn a new language in an immersion setting.**
    It takes one to two years to develop social communicative competence in a new language, but five to seven years to achieve high academic proficiency. I hope this exercise has been not only eye-opening but reassuring for you.

You *can* learn to communicate with the people you have been called to serve using a new language. It will take a long time, but it doesn't have to be debilitatingly frustrating. In fact, it can be rewarding. You won't sound like a native speaker, but you don't need to. What matters is that you will be able to share Christ's love using a new language—and you will be able to do that!

What Kind of Language Learner Are You?

In chapters 1 and 2, I corrected some misconceptions that people have about learning a new language, and we also looked at principles of language acquisition. I set out to debunk the idea that "some people just can't learn languages," and instead I put forward the notion of knowing and utilizing your areas of strength. There are many, many ways in which learners might be different, but one of the more obvious areas of difference involves what I call "language strength" versus "communication strength." Though a person might have strengths in both of these areas, it is often the case that a person leans toward one or the other.

Check the following statements that are most like you, in order to see if your greater area of strength is "language" or "communication."

Language Strength
   ____ I like to study grammar and figure out how language works.
   ____ I am a good speller and editor in my native language.
   ____ I like to get things right; it's important to me to use the right words and grammar.

_____ I like traditional learning methods; for example, I enjoy filling out worksheets when I know what to do.

_____ What I least enjoy is having to say something on the spur of the moment—when I haven't had a chance to plan and practice what I will say.

Communication Strength

_____ I like to talk to people.

_____ If I'm able to get my idea across, it doesn't really bother me if my language isn't correct.

_____ I would much rather be out, and using the language, than in a classroom learning it.

_____ I don't mind asking people to repeat or rephrase; I want to make sure I understand.

_____ What I least enjoy is going through a grammar book or filling out worksheets.

It is important for much of your language study to utilize your area of strength. If you really enjoy learning the grammar, you need a good grammar book and a teacher who can explain what you don't understand. If your strength lies more in communication, you will want to spend a lot of time interacting with people, learning the new language from them rather than just in the classroom. That said, both types of learners will need to engage in their areas of weakness in order to learn a new language. The learner with *language strength* will still need to communicate with people, and the learner with *communication strength* will also need to learn some concepts and rules about the new language.

Fortunately, we can use our strengths to build bridges into the areas in which we are less comfortable. For example, the learner with "language strength" can be afforded a lot of time to plan, practice, and rehearse before being asked to talk to someone outside the classroom. And the learner who feels much more comfortable outside of the classroom can perhaps be inspired in the classroom by learning phrases that are very practical and colloquial, which anyone he meets is likely to understand and respond to positively.

What Are Your Language Learning Goals?

Different types of ministry may require different types and levels of competence in the new language. If you will be teaching graduate level courses in the language, you will likely need very high, academic-level language in reading, writing, speaking, and listening. But if you will be teaching in an English-medium school, you may primarily need oral communicative competence and very specific literacy skills, such as the ability to fill out forms or read familiar passages in the Bible.

It can be helpful to utilize an established language proficiency scale as you set your goals. See appendix E for several widely used proficiency scales. Your organization may use one of these, or have their own descriptors based on one of these.

The chart below provides a brief description of oral and written proficiency at basic, intermediate, and advanced levels. Use this chart to begin thinking about your goals, in connection with your future intended ministry. Setting some broad goals can help you focus your language learning in the areas you most want to develop.

Language Learning Goals (Check all goals that apply)

	Goal statement	Goal description
	Basic oral communicative competence	Can communicate orally (speaking and listening) in informal settings on familiar topics
	Basic written communicative competence	Can read basic words and communicate basic ideas in writing on familiar topics (e.g., texting, reading signs, reading and writing lists, etc.)
	Intermediate level oral proficiency	Can communicate orally in more formal social settings such as a classroom, and can accomplish oral tasks in public such as getting directions, making purchases, etc.
	Intermediate level literacy	Can read intermediate level texts, or known texts, such as the Bible. Can write informal texts such as emails, and short paragraphs on known topics.
	Advanced oral proficiency	Can understand complex and/or academic language, such as in a lecture or sermon. Can communicate orally using academic language and complex structures.
	Advanced literacy	Can learn new academic content through reading, and enjoys reading for pleasure. Can write academic texts such as reports and essays.

What Kind of Program Do You Need?

Knowing yourself as a learner and identifying your language learning goals are good first steps in identifying the type of language program that is best for you. But many other factors come into play as well. In chapters 3 and 4 we looked at "formal" vs. "informal" language study options and posed a series of questions that could be used in decision-making. Here, various factors are brought together into one resource, which may help guide your thought process.

Decision-making flow chart:
Is there a reputable formal language school option?

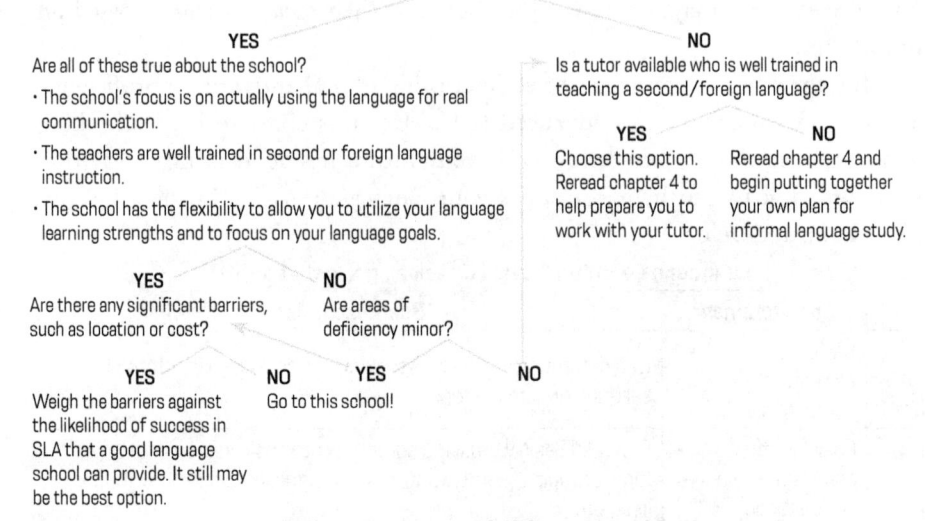

YES
Are all of these true about the school?
- The school's focus is on actually using the language for real communication.
- The teachers are well trained in second or foreign language instruction.
- The school has the flexibility to allow you to utilize your language learning strengths and to focus on your language goals.

NO
Is a tutor available who is well trained in teaching a second/foreign language?

YES
Choose this option. Reread chapter 4 to help prepare you to work with your tutor.

NO
Reread chapter 4 and begin putting together your own plan for informal language study.

YES
Are there any significant barriers, such as location or cost?

NO
Are areas of deficiency minor?

YES
Weigh the barriers against the likelihood of success in SLA that a good language school can provide. It still may be the best option.

NO
Go to this school!

YES

NO

What Do Your Children Need?

As we saw in chapter 5, when families move overseas for ministry, the needs of the children must be considered. While parents and organizations often do well in processing children's anticipated developmental and educational needs, little attention has sometimes been paid to the *language* needs of the children. How will they learn the local language while continuing to develop their native language? Will they be exposed to or need to learn more than one additional language? This might be the case if the language of schooling is different than the language of ministry—and both are different from the home language. This section provides some tools that may be helpful as you prepare to meet your children's educational and language needs.

What are viable schooling options?

To help process various schooling options, consider creating a chart like the one below. You may need a separate chart for each child if they might need different schooling options. You may want to reread portions of chapter 5 to review some of the characteristics of each type of schooling.

Child: _____

International School	Pros	Cons	Potential for SLA
National School	Pros	Cons	Potential for SLA
Homeschool	Pros	Cons	Potential for SLA

What language goals are appropriate for your children?

It can be helpful to think through your expectations for your children in terms of acquiring the language of your place of ministry, just as you processed your own language goals above. If your children are older, say upper elementary and above, they need to be involved in this goal-setting. Try to be realistic about language goals. If your home language is English and your children will attend an English-medium school, it may not be realistic to set an expectation of learning the local language to an advanced level. Rather, it might be best to focus on gaining communicative competence on a variety of common topics of conversation.

The template on the following page might be useful in envisioning children's language learning goals. For each child, put a checkmark in the left column in regard to all appropriate language goals. In the far right column, put a checkmark beside the means for reaching the goal, or add other envisioned language learning opportunities.

Child: _____ Age: _____

Language Learning Goals (Check all goals that apply)

Goal statement	Goal description	Method of attaining goal
Basic oral communicative competence	Can communicate orally (speaking and listening) in informal settings on familiar topics.	___ House helper or nanny, with *intentional* interaction in the language ___ Tutor at home ___ Foreign language class in an international school ___ National schooling that has an intentional program for initial language development
Basic written communicative competence	Can read basic words and communicate basic ideas in writing, on familiar topics (e.g., texting, reading signs, reading and writing lists, etc.).	___ Tutor at home ___ Foreign language class in an international school ___ National schooling that has an intentional program for initial language development
Intermediate level oral proficiency	Can communicate orally in more formal social settings, such as a classroom; and can accomplish oral tasks in public, such as getting directions, making purchases, etc.	___ Tutor at home ___ Foreign language class in an international school ___ National schooling that has an intentional program for initial language development
Intermediate level literacy	Can read intermediate level texts, or known texts, such as the Bible. Can write informal texts, such as emails, and short paragraphs on known topics.	___ Tutor at home ___ Foreign language class in an international school ___ National schooling that has an intentional program for initial language development
Advanced oral proficiency	Can understand complex and/or academic language, such as in a lecture or sermon. Can communicate orally using academic language and complex structures.	___ Tutor at home ___ Content-based instruction* in an international school or other option ___ National schooling
Advanced literacy	Can learn new academic content through reading, and enjoys reading for pleasure. Can write academic texts, such as reports and essays.	___ Tutor at home ___ Content-based instruction* in an international school or other option ___ National schooling

*Content-based instruction is the use of a foreign language to learn new content. For example, an international school might offer an advanced foreign language option of studying the history of the local language through the medium of the local language. The history would be the "content," but the local language will also be learned to an advanced level because the instruction occurs in that language. Content-based instruction could also be achieved in other ways, such as attending a Bible study in the local language.

Applying New Understanding to Chart a Path for Success

How will your language study impact your children?
Imagine that you are planning to send your children to an excellent international school, where they will be using their native language for instruction, and the curriculum will be familiar to them. Their teachers have been trained in your home country, and your children will feel comfortable with them. Further, they will be at school all day and you will have time to get all of your own language school homework done before they arrive home. Family life will go on pretty much like it did in your home country, right? WRONG! Even with all of these "ideal" conditions, your children are still in a new school. They still have new routines. And most of all—you are still in a brand-new country and culture, hearing a brand-new language.

There will be issues, problems, and challenges, no matter how "ideal" the context. And many contexts are not as "ideal" as the one I just described. How can you best chart a course for your language study time that won't negatively impact your family? Here are some suggestions:

1. Create solid family routines before you go to the field, and keep them diligently once you are there. One such important routine is family devotions. This was a nonnegotiable family activity when I was growing up, and I remember family devotions as a time of calm and security during the year my parents were in language school. Rod and I carried on this tradition with our own daughters, and they too have spoken about how this regular family time, reconnecting us with God and each other at the end of the day, was a steadying force during our years in Indonesia, Brazil, and then back to Indonesia. It was always a predictable time of family togetherness, no matter what difficulties we were facing.

2. Consider how your children's needs and your own language study needs will mesh. If you are attending a language school, will homework be assigned? If so, will you have time to do it when the children are otherwise occupied? Or do you need a language study program where there is no homework? Can you and your spouse alternate times with the children and times in individual language study? Will your children be attending a school in which they will be assigned a lot of homework requiring parental assistance? Such questions can sometimes be asked and understood in advance. For example, if your children will be attending international or national schooling, you can ask in advance about the school's homework policy, so you will know what to expect and how to plan. If you are homeschooling, can you create family language study times with a tutor coming to the house?

3. Prepare for the emotional impact of learning a new language. Learning a new language is stressful, as well as physically and emotionally exhausting. And so is moving, being in a new culture, going to a new school, eating new food…. The stress factors can really pile up during your first couple of years in your new place of ministry. How will you de-stress, both individually and as a family? How frequently might you want to plan to talk with family and friends back home, as an opportunity to help you balance the need to de-stress and stay connected with the need to still focus on acculturating to your new environment? Are you taking with you some helpful de-stressors for yourself and your children, such as books and craft supplies? A common go-to for de-stressing is TV, movies, and video games. To what extent will these resources be healthy and helpful? Thinking through these questions before you go can be helpful. We tried to limit movie-watching to the weekends, and to use other means of de-stressing, such as reading books during the week. This proved to be a healthy balance for our family—and our daughters became avid readers!

4. Ensure the health of your marriage. We all know that having a healthy marriage is one of the best things you can do for your children. But language learning can stretch your marriage to its limits! Here are a few tips from our experiences:

a. Tread very carefully if you are tempted to help your spouse with the new language. Spousal corrections are often not received with appreciation! This can be especially true if one spouse is making much better progress in learning the language than the other, which often seems to be the case. If you are the more highly proficient spouse, resist the temptation to think that your spouse is just not "doing it right," dedicating enough time to learning, or being motivated enough.

b. Understand that people process all the changes you are going through in different ways. Now that you're in a brand-new environment, you may see sides of your spouse that you didn't know were there and which prompt different reactions than you've seen before. Accept this "new" person, and embrace the opportunity to learn more about each other.

c. Find time for some of the things you have always enjoyed doing together. Maybe it's time together at a coffee shop after dropping the kids off at school. Maybe it's long walks in nature. You will have to adapt to new schedules and a new environment, but keep a time, at least once a week, to do something together that you both enjoy. And *don't* talk about language learning during this time!

How Can You Envision Your Language Learning Time as Ministry?

We are the salt and light of Christ each day of our lives. We don't put our Christian witness on hold while we're in language school. Hopefully chapter 6 gave you some food for thought as to what type of ministry God may have for you during your time of focused language study. Here are some suggestions that can help you think through this aspect of your time in language learning. Check all that apply, and add others that are relevant in your context.

____ I think I might benefit from spending a few hours each week in some type of ministry in my native language, even though I know my main responsibility will be learning the new language.

Possible ministry opportunities to seek out could be:

____ Leading a Bible study

____ Teaching English

____ Mentoring or coaching

____ Other: _____

____ I would like to look for a language teacher, tutor, or helper who might want to learn more about the Bible by helping me learn the Bible in the new language.

____ I would like to look for a secular language course or program where I could be in contact with teachers and students who aren't Christians, although I'm fully aware that I should maintain the posture of a learner and demonstrate respect for those of different beliefs.

____ I want to purposefully take opportunities to ask questions about the language and culture, prompting both myself and my interlocutors to look together at our cultural practices in light of God's Word.

____ I want to be a humble and transparent learner of the new language and culture. I will try to have intentional interactions in which I can learn from those with whom I interact.

There may be many other ways in which God might use you and your family during this time in which you are focused on learning a new language and culture. The purpose of this exercise is to envision various ways in which your language learning time might include ministry, so that you can identify situations that might work well for you and be alert for open doors that God may have for you.

Conclusion

As you prepare to move to a new culture and learn a new language, you are embarking on an experience that will change you and your family in dramatic ways. As you remain faithful to God, implementing the knowledge you now have, he will not only enable you to learn the new language, but will bless you and your family through this phase and beyond. I am eternally grateful that my parents did not give up and return to the States when language learning was hard. And I am so grateful that they gave me opportunities to learn Portuguese, even though it was hard. God will sustain you, empower you, and use the challenges for his glory.

"He who began a good work in you will carry it on to completion until the day of Christ Jesus."—Philippians 1:6

REFERENCES

Bailey, F. and K. Pransky. 2013. "Implications and Applications of the Latest Brain Research for English Language Learners and Teachers." Webinar provided by TESOL International Association.

Bialystok, E., and K. Hakuta. 1994. *In Other Words: The Science and Psychology of Second-Language Acquisition*. New York: Basic Books.

Brown, H. D. and H. Lee. 2015. *Teaching by Principles: An Interactive Approach to Language Pedagogy*. 4th ed. White Plains, NY: Pearson.

Chomsky, N. 1959. "Review of *Verbal Behavior*, by B. F. Skinner." *Language* 35, no. 1: 26–58.

Collier, V. P. 1989. "How Long? A Synthesis of Research on Academic Achievement in a Second Language." *TESOL Quarterly* 23: 509–31.

Collier, V. P., and W. P. Thomas. 2004. "The astounding effectiveness of dual language education for all." *NABE Journal of Research and Practice*, 21.

Creese, A., and A. Blackledge. 2010. "Translanguaging in The Bilingual Classroom: A Pedagogy For Learning And Teaching?" *The Modern Language Journal* 94, no. 1: 103–115.

Cummins, J. 1981. "The Role of Primary Language Development in Promoting Educational Success for Language Minority Students." In *Schooling and Language Minority Students: A Theoretical Framework*. Los Angeles: California State University, Evaluation, Dissemination and Assessment Center, 3–49.

Cummins, J. 2000. *Language, Power, and Pedagogy: Bilingual Children in the Crossfire*. Clevedon, England: Multilingual Matters.

Dormer, J. E. 2009. "Language Development for MKs." *Evangelical Missions Quarterly* 45, no. 2 (April): 188–96.

——— (2011). *Teaching English in Missions: Effectiveness and Integrity*. Pasadena, CA: William Carey Library Publishers.

Gaither, M. 2017. *Homeschool: An American History*. 2nd ed. London: Palgrave Macmillan.

García, O., and L. Wei. 2013. *Translanguaging: Language, Bilingualism and Education*. Basingstoke, United Kingdom: Palgrave Macmillan.

Genesee, F. 2007. "A Short Guide to Raising Children Bilingually." *Multilingual Living Magazine*, http://www.psych.mcgill.ca/perpg/fac/genesee/A%20Short%20 Guide%20to%20Raising%20Children%20Bilingually.pdf.

Hakuta, K., E. Bialystok, and E. Wiley. 2003. "Critical Evidence: A Test of The Critical-Period Hypothesis For Second-Language Acquisition." *Psychological Science*, 14, no. 1: 31–38.

Hartshorne, J. K., J. B. Tenenbaum, and S. Pinker. 2018. "A Critical Period for Second Language Acquisition: Evidence from 2/3 Million English Speakers." *Cognition*. Vol. 177 (August): 263–77. https://doi.org/10.1016/j.cognition.2018.04.007.

Krashen, S. 1981. *Second Language Acquisition and Second Language Learning.* New York: Pergamon.

Kuhl, P. K. 2010. "Brain Mechanisms in Early Language Acquisition." *Neuron* 67, no. 5: 713–27.

Lightbown, P .M. & Spada, N. (2013). *How Languages are Learned.* 4th. Ed. Oxford University Press. Oxford, UK. ISBN #13 978194541268

Long, M. H. (1997). "Focus on Form in Task-Based Language Teaching." www.mhhe.com. McGraw-Hill Companies.

Nation, I. S .P., & Newton, J. M. (2020). *Teaching ESL/EFL Listening and Speaking* (ESL & Applied Linguistics Professional Series) 2nd Edition. Routledge. ISBN-13: 978-0367195519

Nation, I. S. P., & Macalister, J. (2020). *Teaching ESL/EFL Reading and Writing* (ESL & Applied Linguistics Professional Series) 2nd Edition. Routledge. ISBN-13: 978-0367433772.

Ramirez, J. D., S. D. Yuen, and D. R. Ramey. 1991. "Longitudinal Study of Structured English Immersion Strategy: Early-Exit and Late-Exit Transitional Bilingual Education Programs For Language Minority Children." *Final Report.* Volumes 1 and 2. San Mateo, CA: Aguirre International.

Smith, D. I., and B. Carvill. 2000. *The Gift of the Stranger: Faith, Hospitality and Foreign Language Learning.* Grand Rapids: Eerdmans.

Snow, C., and M. Hoefnagel-Hohle. 1982. "The Critical Period for Language Acquisition: Evidence from Second Language Learning." In *Issues in Second Language Research.* Edited by S. Krashen, R. Scarcell, and M. Long, 93–113. London: Newbury House.

Snow, D. 2001. *English Teaching as Christian Mission: An Applied Theology.* Scottdale, PA: Herald Press.

Swain, M. (1985) *Communicative Competence: Some Roles of Comprehensible Input And Comprehensible Output In Its Development.* In Gass, S. and Madden, C. (Eds.), *Input in Second Language Acquisition*, 235–56. New York: Newbury House.

Taylor, F. 2013. *Self and Identity in Adolescent Foreign Language Learning.* Bristol, United Kingdom: Multilingual Matters.

Vanhove J. 2013. "The Critical Period Hypothesis in Second Language Acquisition: A Statistical Critique and a Reanalysis." *PloS one* 8, no. 7. e69172. doi:10.1371/journal.pone.0069172.

Vygotsky, L. S. (1978). *Mind In Society: The Development Of Higher Psychological Processes.* Cambridge, MA: Harvard University Press.

Wrobbel, K. A. 2008. "Are National Schools A Viable Option?" *Evangelical Missions Quarterly* 44: 70–77.

———. 2016. "From National School to U.S. College." *Evangelical Missions Quarterly* 52, no. 3: 248–54.

APPENDIX

Language Proficiency Scales

Various language proficiency models are provided below. Others can be found through an online search for "language proficiency models" or "language proficiency scales."

TESOL (Teaching English to Speakers of Other Languages)

TESOL International Association provides a description of general language abilities in five levels in its *Pre-K-12 English Language Proficiency Standards Framework*. Though these descriptions were written for K-12 education, they can be applied to language learners of any age.

Level 1—Starting

At Level 1, students initially have limited or no understanding of English. They rarely use English for communication. They respond nonverbally to simple commands, statements, and questions. As their oral comprehension increases, they begin to imitate the verbalizations of others by using single words or simple phrases, and they begin to use English spontaneously. At the earliest stage, these learners construct meaning from text primarily through illustrations, graphs, maps, and tables.

Level 2—Emerging

At Level 2, students can understand phrases and short sentences. They can communicate limited information in simple everyday and routine situations by using memorized phrases, groups of words, and formulae. They can use selected simple structures correctly but still systematically produce basic errors. Students begin to use general academic vocabulary and familiar everyday expressions. Errors in writing are present that often hinder communication.

Level 3—Developing

At Level 3, students understand more complex speech but still may require some repetition. They use English spontaneously but may have difficulty expressing all their thoughts due to a restricted vocabulary and a limited command of language structure. Students at this level speak in simple sentences, which are comprehensible and appropriate, but which are frequently marked by grammatical errors. Proficiency in reading may vary considerably. Students are most successful constructing meaning from texts for which they have background knowledge upon which to build.

Level 4—Expanding

At Level 4, students' language skills are adequate for most day-to-day communication needs. They communicate in English in new or unfamiliar settings but have occasional difficulty with complex structures and abstract academic concepts. Students at this level may read with considerable fluency and are able to locate and identify the specific facts within the text. However, they may not understand texts in which the concepts are presented in a decontextualized manner, the sentence structure is complex, or the vocabulary is abstract or has multiple meanings. They can read independently but may have occasional comprehension problems, especially when processing grade-level information.

Level 5—Bridging

At Level 5, students can express themselves fluently and spontaneously on a wide range of personal, general, academic, or social topics in a variety of contexts. They are poised to function in an environment with native speaking peers with minimal language support or guidance. Students have a good command of technical and academic vocabulary as well of idiomatic expressions and colloquialisms. They can produce clear, smoothly flowing, well-structured texts of differing lengths and degrees of linguistic complexity. Errors are minimal, difficult to spot, and generally corrected when they occur.

(Descriptions of the TESOL level descriptors are taken from *TESOL Pre-K-12 English Language Proficiency Standards Framework,* available at http://www.tesol.org/docs/books/bk_prek-12elpstandards_framework_318.pdf?sfvrsn=2.)

ACTFL (American Council of Teachers of Foreign Languages)

This organization proposes an 11-level set of descriptors of language proficiency. The ACTFL model of language proficiency levels is provided below, and detailed descriptions of language abilities can be found at: https://www.actfl.org/about-the-american-council-the-teaching-foreign-languages. ACTFL can be a very useful resource in language learning, as their site provides information in various languages, as well as videos showing language learners at various levels of proficiency.

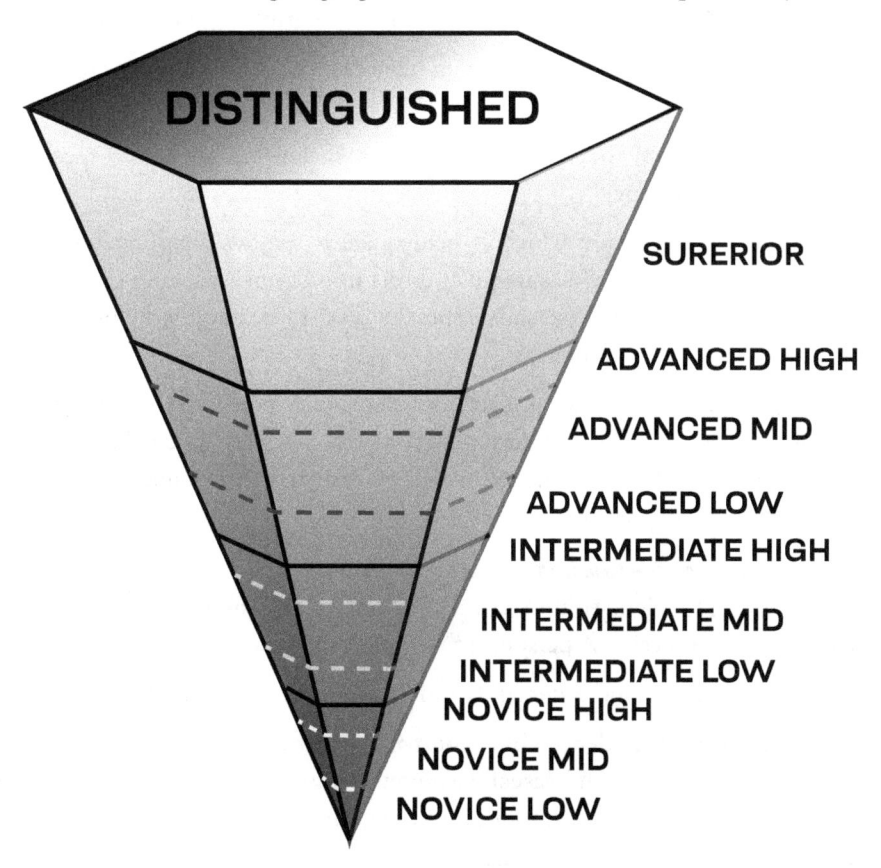

- DISTINGUISHED
- SURERIOR
- ADVANCED HIGH
- ADVANCED MID
- ADVANCED LOW
- INTERMEDIATE HIGH
- INTERMEDIATE MID
- INTERMEDIATE LOW
- NOVICE HIGH
- NOVICE MID
- NOVICE LOW

FSI (Foreign Service Institute)

The U.S. Foreign Service utilizes a five-level framework to identify language proficiency levels. Descriptions of these levels are provided here:

Foreign service level 1—Elementary proficiency
Elementary proficiency is the first level in the scale. This level is sometimes referred to as S-1 or level 1. A person at this level is described as follows:

- able to satisfy routine travel needs and minimum courtesy requirements
- can ask and answer questions on very familiar topics; within the scope of very limited language experience
- can understand simple questions and statements, allowing for slowed speech, repetition or paraphrase
- has a speaking vocabulary which is inadequate to express anything but the most elementary needs; makes frequent errors in pronunciation and grammar, but can be understood by a native speaker used to dealing with foreigners attempting to speak the language
- while topics which are "very familiar" and elementary needs vary considerably from individual to individual, any person at the S-1 level should be able to order a simple meal, ask for shelter or lodging, ask and give simple directions, make purchases, and tell time.

Foreign service level 2—Limited working proficiency
Limited working proficiency is the second level in the scale. This level is sometimes referred to as S-2 or level 2. A person at this level is described as follows:

- able to satisfy routine social demands and limited work requirements
- can handle with confidence, but not with facility, most social situations including introductions and casual conversations about current events, as well as work, family, and autobiographical information
- can handle limited work requirements, needing help in handling any complications or difficulties; can get the gist of most conversations on non-technical subjects (i.e. topics which require no specialized knowledge), and has a speaking vocabulary sufficient to respond simply with some circumlocutions
- has an accent which, though often quite faulty, is intelligible
- can usually handle elementary constructions quite accurately but does not have thorough or confident control of the grammar.

Appendix A: Language Proficiency Scales

Foreign service level 3—Professional working proficiency
Professional working proficiency is the third level in the scale. This level is sometimes referred to as S-3 or level 3. S-3 is what is usually used to measure how many people in the world know a given language. A person at this level is described as follows:
- able to speak the language with sufficient structural accuracy and vocabulary to participate effectively in most formal and informal conversations on practical, social, and professional topics
- can discuss particular interests and special fields of competence with reasonable ease
- has comprehension which is quite complete for a normal rate of speech
- has a general vocabulary which is broad enough that he or she rarely has to grope for a word
- has an accent which may be obviously foreign; has a good control of grammar; and whose errors virtually never interfere with understanding and rarely disturb the native speaker.

Foreign service level 4—Full professional proficiency
Full professional proficiency is the fourth level in the scale. This level is sometimes referred to as S-4 or level 4. A person at this level is described as follows:
- able to use the language fluently and accurately on all levels normally pertinent to professional needs
- can understand and participate in any conversations within the range of own personal and professional experience with a high degree of fluency and precision of vocabulary
- would rarely be taken for a native speaker, but can respond appropriately even in unfamiliar situations
- makes only quite rare and unpatterned errors of pronunciation and grammar
- can handle informal interpreting from and into the language.

Foreign service level 5—Native or bilingual proficiency
Native or bilingual proficiency is the fifth level in the scale. This level is sometimes referred to as S-5 or level 5. A person at this level is described as follows:
- has a speaking proficiency equivalent to that of an educated native speaker has; complete fluency in the language, such that speech on all levels is fully accepted by educated native speakers in all of its features, including breadth of vocabulary and idiom, colloquialisms, and pertinent cultural references.

More information on the Foreign Service Institute, including estimated times for learning various languages, can be found at https://www.state.gov/foreign-language-training/.

CEFR (Common European Framework of Reference)

In Europe, the CEFR framework is the most commonly used in describing language proficiency levels. It is summarized in the following chart:

PROFICIENT USER	C2	Can understand with ease virtually everything heard or read. Can sumarise information from different spoken and written sources, reconstructing arguments and accounts in a coherent presentation. Can express him/herself spontaneously, very fluently and precisely, differentiating finer shades of meaning even in more complex situations.
	C1	Can understand a wide range of demanding, longer texts, and recognise implicit meaning. Can express him/herself fluently and spontaneously, without much obvious searching for expressions. Can use language flexibly and effectively for social and academic and professional purposes. Can produce clear, well-structured, detailed text on complex subjects, showing controlled use of organisational patterns, connectors and cohesive devices.
INDEPENDENT USER	B2	Can understand the main ideas of complex text on both concrete and abstract topics, including technical discussions in his/her field of specialisation. Can interact with a degree of fluency and spontaneity that makes regular interaction with native speakers quite possible without strain for either party. Can produce clear, detailed text on a wide range of subjects and explain a viewpoint on a topical issue giving the advantages and disadvantages of various options.
	B1	Can understand the main points of clear standard input on familiar matters regularly encountered in work, school, leisure, etc. Can deal with most situations likely to arise whilst traveling in an area where the language is spoken. Can produce simple connected text on topics which are familiar or of personal interest. Can describe experiences and events, dreams, hopes & ambitions and briefly give reasons and explanations or opinions or plans.
BASIC USER	A2	Can understand sentences and frequently used expressions related to areas of most immediate relevance (e.g. very basic personal and family information, shopping, local geography, employment.) Can communicate in simple and routine tasks requiring a simple and direct exchange of information on familiar and routine matters. Can describe in simple terms aspects of his/her background, immediate environment and matters in areas of immediate need.
	A1	Can understand and use familiar everyday expressions and very basic phrases aimed at the satisfaction of needs of a concrete type. Can introduce him/herself and others and can ask and answer questions about personal details such as where he/she lives, people he/she knows and things he/she has. Can interact in a simple way provided the other person talks slowly and clearly and is prepared to help.

For more information about CEFR, including descriptions in other languages, see https://www.coe.int/en/web/common-european-framework-reference-languages/level-descriptions.

Other Frameworks

Many other frameworks to describe proficiency levels are available. Some of these include:

WIDA

This is a set of standards used in K-12 education. The six WIDA language levels are described specifically in reference to the English language capabilities of children who are learning English within English-medium schools. The standards are identified by proficiency levels, grade levels, and academic subjects. See https://wida.wisc.edu/

Canadian Language Benchmarks

This set of level descriptors was created specifically to describe adult English language learning in language programs for new Canadians.

See https://www.language.ca/home/

English for life

This is my own five-level, task-based curriculum (see appendix B). Though it does not include descriptors at each level, the checklists for each of the five levels can serve as level assessments or goals.

APPENDIX B

English for Life Curriculum

What Is English for Life?

English for Life is a five-level curriculum for adult and teen learners of English as a foreign language (EFL). It is based on task checklists referred to as Ability Checklists. The program includes projects, but not a textbook. More information and the curriculum guidelines are available by contacting me at jan.dormer@gmail.com. Here I provide an introduction and the task checklists. These checklists may be used without charge and without requesting permission. Any one of the levels may serve as a curriculum guide for a course. All five levels together may serve as a basis for a full English program.

Introduction

Central to the idea of *English for Life* is the notion that the best teacher of language is a person, not a book. This approach was born through dissatisfaction with the perspective that many teachers and learners seem to have that "going through the book" is the goal of a language class.

The *English for Life* system stresses class content that is:

Communicative: Use language for *real communication* through reading, writing, speaking, and listening.
Contextualized: Use language for *local* purposes. Talk about *learners' lives*.
Edifying: Use language to stimulate positive *growth* in learners and teachers.

Appendix B: English for Life Curriculum

Contextualization

To change the material in many English learning programs is to break copyright laws. Not so with *English for Life*! The system is available digitally so that teachers can change and adapt it for their own contexts. Currently these materials are prepared for the Indonesian context. What language is learned and how it is learned, in *your* context, should be determined by student realities and needs. Teachers and students should use what is given here as a starting point, and then adapt it to meet their needs.

Christian Perspective

My goal through this curriculum is to achieve excellence in language teaching while encouraging the use of Christian content where appropriate. *English for Life* has been used in situations in which learners aren't Christians but are open to developing friendships with Christian teachers and learning about Christian beliefs. It has also been used with Christian students as a springboard for discipleship and leadership development. With this material, teachers and students can pick and choose the elements and materials that are appropriate. Some examples of Christian elements are:

- A Bible memory program: Each checklist includes the Scripture that is learned at that level. If this isn't appropriate for a given context, it can be removed.

- Inclusion of Christians in job descriptions (for example, a banker who is a Christian).

- Inclusion of both Christian and secular curriculum options. For example, in level five teachers can choose to use either a "personality test" or a "spiritual gifts inventory."

- Learning to say a prayer of blessing when learning about mealtimes.

Themes

The thematic content for each level is as follows:

Summary of Content

Level	Focus	Content
Level 1	Basic Vocabulary and Phrases	Greetings, food, home, family, numbers and money, community
Level 2	Home and Family	Introductions, descriptions, jobs, home life, house, schedules and habits
Level 3	Community	The neighborhood, stores, services, directions, professions
Level 4	The World	Culture, customs, holidays, geography, countries
Level 5	Personal Development	Spiritual life, traditions, beliefs, worldview, spiritual truth, missions

Completion Goals
After completing all five levels of *English for Life,* a student should be able to:
- Talk easily and fluently about family, self, city, and country, and express personal opinions. The student may have errors, but will be able to communicate effectively.
- Understand personal information shared by others, and ask pertinent questions.
- Ask for clarification when necessary, demonstrate when he or she does not understand, and continue communication until comprehension is achieved.
- Give and understand social information, such as directions, time, spelling of words, descriptions, costs, quality, etc.
- Read and gain a general understanding about worldwide information, such as news articles, information on the internet, or letters received from friends.
- Accomplish basic writing tasks, such as writing friendly letters or recipes, although writing will likely have some grammatical errors.

Overview
Each of the five levels includes eight topical units (level one has ten). Grammar is not addressed specifically in this curriculum, but rather will be learned as a by-product of the topical tasks. If more grammar instruction is desired, a basic grammar book can be used alongside this curriculum, beginning in level two. I prefer to focus on vocabulary acquisition with incidental grammar learning in level one. My recommendations for grammar texts are *Basic Grammar in Use* (levels 2–4) and *Grammar in Use Intermediate* (level 5) both by Raymond Murphy (2017 and 2018, Cambridge Press).

I suggest that each unit covers two weeks of instruction, or eight hours of classroom time. Curriculum guidelines for each level are available separately via my email address. These provide some activities and resources for each topical unit at each level. However, it is important that teachers who use this curriculum understand that it is meant to be contextualized by using materials brought in and/or created by both teacher and students.

Recycling
An important feature of this curriculum is that content is "recycled" and revisited at different levels, in different ways. For example, on the topic of food:

    Level 1: students learn names of foods
    Level 2: students revisit names of foods, talk about food preferences and diet, and learn to read simple recipes

Level 3: students talk about food again as they learn to order a meal at a restaurant
Level 4: students compare diets and nutrition in various countries

Students who have opportunities to review, remember, and build on previous learning in such ways are usually more successful in long-term language acquisition.

Projects

My hope is that students and teachers engaged in the *English for Life* system will find that their time in class is spent not only learning English but engaging in meaningful, interesting, and relevant activities. To promote this concept, a semester-long class project for each level (after level 1) is suggested. The project activities are inherent in the units, making it possible for students to finish the level having created something that is useful. Here are some suggested projects for each level:

Level 2: Home and Family: A booklet for foreigners about Indonesian families and their homes.
Level 3: Community: A booklet for foreigners providing tips for living in Indonesia.
Level 4: The World: A video presentation of different areas of the world.
Level 5: Personal Development: Individual portfolios of personal growth and expectations.

Many other projects are possible. Local contexts and student interests should determine what of lasting value can be accomplished in a semester.

A General Understanding of Tasks

The list of tasks for each level is provided in the Ability Checklist. Students receive this checklist at the beginning of the semester, and teachers plan their lessons using the suggested activities and materials in the curriculum guidelines or developing their own activities and materials. Class activities should be designed with the purpose of enabling students to check off the "I can" statements on their checklist. Here is an example of teaching activities to accompany the curriculum:

Task examples from Level 3:

I can *give directions* to well-known places in my city.

I can *understand* directions and *write* them down.

1. Provide a map of the school campus. In pairs, have students practice giving instructions to each other regarding how to find their English class when they come on campus: turn right/left; go straight/up/down; first door on the right, etc.

2. Have students work in groups to prepare written instructions to get from the school to some well-known places in town. Have students compile these written instructions to create a document that would be helpful for a foreigner.

3. Have students work in pairs, taking turns giving and writing down how to get from the school to their homes.

Integration of Skill Areas
This system promotes the integration of reading, writing, speaking, and listening wherever possible. The wording of student tasks sometimes promotes two skill areas, as in the task above: "I can *understand* (listening) directions and *write* (writing) them down." But skill integration can also be accomplished by developing class activities which accomplish several tasks. Ideas for this type of integration are provided in the curriculum guides. Teachers will no doubt expand on these ideas, finding additional ways to integrate the four skill areas. For instance, on the subject of Indonesian holidays, various tasks encourage students, in effect, to "read, write, and speak about an Indonesian holiday." The sequence below illustrates one way to integrate these skills in classroom activities:

Students will ...

- Write a paragraph about a holiday; teacher provides input for student correction

- Exchange paragraphs and read; write three follow-up questions

- Answer questions orally

- Tell a friend about the holiday

Assessment
This system promotes learner autonomy and relies on self-assessment as the primary means of evaluation. Students decide at what point they feel comfortable checking off items on the Ability Checklists stating that they indeed *can* do those tasks in English. In many places self-assessment is new for learners, so this system works best accompanied by periodic one-on-one progress meetings with the teacher. These meetings can include student evaluation of their effort in the class and their view of their progress in each of the language skill areas. This system may not be the most ideal if formal tests and grades must be given.

Appendix B: English for Life Curriculum

Ability Checklist Level 1: Basic Words and Phrases

Name: _____ Dates: _____

1. **Greetings and Phrases**
   - ☐ I know these greetings: *hello, good morning, good afternoon, good evening.*
   - ☐ I know these words and phrases: *please, thank you, you're welcome.*

   I know this dialogue:
   - ☐ A: *Hi, how are you?*
   - ☐ B: *I'm fine, how are you?*
   - ☐ A: *I'm fine.*

   I know this dialogue:
   - ☐ A: *My name is _____. What's your name?*
   - ☐ B: *My name is _____.*
   - ☐ A: *Nice to meet you.*
   - ☐ I know how to say *goodbye.*
   - ☐ I know these phrases: *I don't speak English yet. I don't understand. Please repeat.*

2. **Letters and Numbers**
   - ☐ I can say the letters of the alphabet.
   - ☐ I can spell my full name.
   - ☐ I can say and understand phone numbers.
   - ☐ I can count to 100.
   - ☐ I can look at a number up to 100,000 and say it.
   - ☐ I can understand and say amounts of money.
   - ☐ I can ask the question *"How much is it?"* and provide the correct amount.

3. **Basic Words**
   - ☐ I know these words and phrases: *yes, no, more-or-less, not yet, maybe.*
   - ☐ I know these colors: yellow, orange, pink, red, green, blue, purple, black, brown, grey, white.
   - ☐ I can describe a color as *light* or *dark.*
   - ☐ I know these words: *big, little, good, bad, happy, sad, tired, busy, hungry, thirsty, clean, dirty, late.*
   - ☐ I know these words: *this, that, these, those.*
   - ☐ I know the basic pronouns, and the verb *to be.*
     Ex: *I am, you are, he/she/it is, we are, you are, they are*
   - ☐ I know these words: *where, when, how, why, who, how much/how many.*

4. **People**
    - ☐ I know these words: *man, woman, child, children, boy, girl.*
    - ☐ I know these *family* words: *mother, father, sister, brother, son, daughter, husband, wife.*
    - ☐ I know these *profession* words: *teacher, student, pastor, doctor* (and words suggested by student).

5. **Days and Months**
    - ☐ I can say the days of the week and the months of the year.
    - ☐ I can use these words: *today, tomorrow, yesterday, day after tomorrow, day before yesterday.*
    - ☐ I can understand and answer the question, *"What day is it today?"*
    - ☐ I can ask and answer the question, *"When is your birthday?"*
    - ☐ I can say and understand years (1985, 2006, etc.).

6. **Food**
    - ☐ I can name ten or more common vegetables.
    - ☐ I can name ten or more common fruits.
    - ☐ I know these words for drinks: *water, milk, soft drinks, juice, tea, coffee.*
    - ☐ I know these words for ingredients: *flour, sugar, oil, butter, salt, pepper.*
    - ☐ I know these words: *meat, chicken, beef, pork, fish, eggs, rice, cake, cookies, bread, pasta.*
    - ☐ I know the words for meal times: *breakfast, lunch, supper/dinner, snack.*

7. **Clothes and Weather**
    - ☐ I know these words: *shirt, T-shirt, pants, shorts, skirt, dress, underwear, socks, swimsuit, jacket.*
    - ☐ I know these words: *hat, shoes, sandals, umbrella, sunglasses, belt, watch, ring, necklace.*
    - ☐ I can describe what I am wearing or what someone else is wearing.
    - ☐ I know these words: *sun, rain, wind, hot, cold, wet, dry.*
    - ☐ I can describe the weather today.
    - ☐ I can relate the weather to what I am wearing.

8. **Activities and Times**
    - ☐ I know these words: *soccer, tennis, swimming, volleyball, basketball, running, walking.*
    - ☐ I know these words: *reading, sewing, watching TV, listening to music, playing guitar/piano, writing letters, cooking.*
    - ☐ I can say the *time.*
    - ☐ I can say what time I do various activities.
    - ☐ I can understand what time someone else does various activities.

9. **House**
    - ☐ I know these words: *living room, dining room, bedroom, bathroom, kitchen, laundry room floor, wall, window, door, ceiling, fan, light.*
    - ☐ I know these *living room & dining room* words: *sofa, chair, TV, desk, computer, table.*
    - ☐ I know these *bedroom* words: *bed, closet, dresser, desk, sheets, blanket, pillow.*
    - ☐ I know these *kitchen* words: *sink, refrigerator, stove, microwave, counter, cabinets.*
    - ☐ I know these *utensil* words: *plate, fork, knife, spoon, bowl, cup, glass, napkin.*
    - ☐ I know these *bathroom* words: *toilet, shower, mirror, towel, soap, toothbrush/ paste, shampoo.*
10. **Body**
    - ☐ I know these words: *face, eyes, ears, nose, mouth, teeth, hair, head.*
    - ☐ I know these words: *arm, hand, fingers, leg, foot, toes, chest, stomach, heart.*
    - ☐ I can say when something hurts. Ex: *I have a headache. My stomach hurts.*
    - ☐ I can understand when someone tells what is wrong with them.

Verbs to learn throughout the course:
- ☐ I know these words: *sit, stand, walk, run, open, close, do, take, give, pray, go, come.*
- ☐ I know these words: *read, write, work, study, try, remember, speak, listen, understand.*
- ☐ I can understand commands or requests using simple verbs.
- ☐ I can make simple sentences about my activities or ideas.
  Ex: *I'm reading. I don't understand.*
- ☐ I know these words: *clean, wash, cook, iron, fix, use, prepare, tidy/straighten, make, buy.*
- ☐ I know how to make a request.
  Ex: *Please cook the meat. Please buy some vegetables.*

Ability Checklist Level 2: Home and Family

Name: _____ Dates: _____

1. **My Family and Me**
    - ☐ I can *fill out* a form, giving personal data.
    - ☐ I can *understand* personal questions and *respond* with information.
    - ☐ I can *ask* questions about someone else, and *understand* the answers.
    - ☐ I can *tell* about my family (physical description, age, personality, hobbies).
    - ☐ I can *ask* about someone else's family, and *understand* answers.
    - ☐ I can *write* a paragraph about a family activity (mealtime, shopping, etc.).
    - ☐ I can *read* a classmate's paragraph about a family activity.
    - ☐ **Vocabulary:** I can *label* the people on a family tree (nephew, aunt, etc.).

2. **A Family Event (vacation, move, birth, wedding, illness, funeral, etc.)**
    - ☐ I can show pictures of a family event and *explain* their meaning.
    - ☐ I can look at a classmate's pictures and *ask* questions.
    - ☐ I can *tell* about a family event and *answer* questions.
    - ☐ I can *understand* an event described by someone else, and *ask* questions.
    - ☐ I can *write* a paragraph about a past event.
    - ☐ I can *read* about someone else's event, and *write* follow-up questions.
    - ☐ **Vocabulary:** I know important words for the family events listed above.

3. **Daily and Weekly Routines**
    - ☐ I can *write* my daily or weekly schedule.
    - ☐ I can *read* someone's schedule, and *ask* follow-up questions.
    - ☐ I can *describe* my schedule and *answer* questions.
    - ☐ I can *tell* what I am doing at different times of the day and week.
    - ☐ I can *ask* what others are doing at different times of the day and week.
    - ☐ I can *read* a description of a daily routine and *write* a schedule.
    - ☐ I can *write* a paragraph describing a particular time in my week.
    - ☐ **Vocabulary:** I know words to describe typical daily and weekly activities.

4. **Weather and Clothing**
    - ☐ I can *read* a paragraph about weather.
    - ☐ I can *read* a weather map, and ask and answer questions with a partner.
    - ☐ I can *describe* what people are wearing, and pictures of clothing.
    - ☐ I can *talk* about appropriate clothing for different weather.
    - ☐ I can *write* about changes in weather or dress.
    - ☐ I can *read* about changes in weather or dress, and *write* questions.
    - ☐ **Vocabulary:** I know words to describe weather, temperatures, and clothing.

5. **Leisure Activities**
    - ☐ I can *describe* pictures of leisure activities.
    - ☐ I can *tell* which activities I have or have not done.
    - ☐ I can *ask* which activities someone else has or has not done.
    - ☐ I can *talk* about activities that I will do on the weekend.
    - ☐ I can *discuss* various sports, giving my opinions.
    - ☐ I can *write* a paragraph describing a leisure activity that I enjoy.
    - ☐ I can *read* a description of a leisure activity, and write follow-up questions.
    - ☐ **Vocabulary:** I know words for leisure activities and sports.

6. **Food**
   - ☐ I can *list* my typical daily diet, and *compare* my diet with someone else's.
   - ☐ I can *understand* products and prices in an American grocery flyer.
   - ☐ I can *talk* about my food preferences, and ask questions about someone else's.
   - ☐ I can *talk* about the food preferences of my family.
   - ☐ I can *compliment* someone on their cooking.
   - ☐ I can *read* a simple recipe.
   - ☐ I can *read* about a food, and *answer* questions.
   - ☐ **Vocabulary:** I know at least thirty food names.

7. **House and Home**
   - ☐ I can *describe* my home, including rooms, colors, and special features.
   - ☐ I can *answer* simple questions about my home.
   - ☐ I can *ask* questions about someone's home, and *understand* their answers.
   - ☐ I can *describe* my home in a letter.
   - ☐ I can *understand* and *answer* questions about my home in a letter.
   - ☐ I can *identify* common household items.
   - ☐ **Vocabulary:** I know words for parts of the house, appliances, and household items.

8. **Friends**
   - ☐ I can *describe* a friend, including looks, personality, and activities.
   - ☐ I can *answer* questions about my friend.
   - ☐ I can *make a polite request*.
   - ☐ I can *extend an invitation*.
   - ☐ I can *interrupt politely*.
   - ☐ I can *make an apology*.
   - ☐ I can *initiate a friendly conversation*.
   - ☐ **Vocabulary:** I know important phrases for the above functions.

Christian Content
   - ☐ I can *recite* the Lord's Prayer.
   - ☐ I can *recite* Psalm 23.
   - ☐ I can *list* benefits of daily family devotions.

Ability Checklist Level 3: Community

Name: _____ Dates: _____

1. **People in the Community**
   - ☐ I can *describe* people who do different jobs (both character and job descriptions).
   - ☐ I can *understand* and *answer* questions about different occupations.
   - ☐ can *read* about different professions, and answer questions.
   - ☐ I can *ask questions* about someone's job, and *answer* questions about my job.
   - ☐ I can *write* a description of my job, or my ideal job.
   - ☐ **Vocabulary:** I know words for many different kinds of occupations.

2. **Living in a Community**
   - ☐ I can *describe* my community or neighborhood in conversation.
   - ☐ I can *ask* questions about someone's community or neighborhood.
   - ☐ I can *take a phone message*.
   - ☐ I can *communicate* in public places, such as the post office or a bank.
   - ☐ I can *read* about common courtesies needed in a community.
   - ☐ **Vocabulary:** I know words for different kinds of stores and transportation.

3. **Maps, Location, Directions**
   - ☐ I can *understand* city signs, and *describe* them in English.
   - ☐ I can *give directions* to important places in my city.
   - ☐ I can *understand* directions and *write* them down.
   - ☐ I can *ask* for help in finding a place when I'm lost; I can *give* help to a stranger.
   - ☐ I can *ask* for clarification when I didn't understand the first time.
   - ☐ **Vocabulary:** I know phrases for giving directions.

4. **Health**
   - ☐ I can *describe* physical symptoms and *ask* for advice.
   - ☐ I can *understand* descriptions of physical symptoms, and *give* advice.
   - ☐ I can *discuss* medicines, and how to take them.
   - ☐ I can *read* about different kinds of exercise, and *write* about my habits.
   - ☐ I can *read* an article about health, *take notes*, and *discuss* it.
   - ☐ I can *share* a prayer request and *pray* about a physical problem.
   - ☐ **Vocabulary:** I know words for health care places, medicines, and conditions.

5. Safety
- ☐ I can *report* an emergency.
- ☐ I can *ask* questions about an emergency, such as address, condition, etc.
- ☐ I can *read* about safety for foreigners in Indonesia, and *tell* a foreigner how to be safe here.
- ☐ I can *write* about a personal experience involving an emergency or safety.
- ☐ I can *read* about someone's experience, and *ask* questions.
- ☐ **Vocabulary:** I know words for emergencies and crimes.

6. Restaurants
- ☐ I can *read* a restaurant menu, and *ask* questions about it.
- ☐ In a restaurant, I can: *order, ask* and *answer* questions, and *ask* for the bill.
- ☐ I can *express* and *understand* food preferences.
- ☐ I can recommend a local restaurant that foreigners might enjoy, in *speaking* and in *writing*.
- ☐ I can *pray* before a meal.
- ☐ **Vocabulary:** I know words and phrases for ordering in a restaurant.

7. Shopping
- ☐ I can *talk* with someone about where and how to buy food.
- ☐ I can *read* product labels, and *ask* questions about products.
- ☐ I can *talk* with sales people in different kinds of stores.
- ☐ I can *understand* a price given in US currency, and give the right amount.
- ☐ I can *participate* in a typical conversation about paying by credit.
- ☐ I can *write* a paragraph related to shopping.
- ☐ I can *read* someone's paragraph, and *write* follow-up questions.
- ☐ **Vocabulary:** I know types of stores, products, and vocabulary about payment.

8. Responsibilities in a Community
- ☐ I can *discuss* civic responsibilities and *tell* about my involvement.
- ☐ I can *understand* and *fill out* an internet volunteer registration form.
- ☐ I can *read* a story about volunteering, and *take notes*.
- ☐ I can *read* about a volunteer opportunity.
- ☐ I can *write* a letter applying for a volunteer position, and answer questions in an interview.
- ☐ I can *compare* volunteering in the US and Indonesia in a *discussion*.
- ☐ I can *give a report* about a local volunteer project, and *answer* questions.
- ☐ **Vocabulary:** I know words related to civic duties and volunteering.

Christian Content
- ☐ I can *recite* John 3:16
- ☐ I can *recite* 1 Corinthians 13:4-8a, 13
- ☐ I can *recite* Galatians 5:22,23a
- ☐ I can *recite* Psalm 121
- ☐ I can *write* about changes and growth in my spiritual life.

Ability Checklist Level 4: The World

Name: _____ Dates: _____

1. International Friendships
- ☐ I can *introduce* myself (past, family, job, etc.) to a foreigner.
- ☐ I can *understand* a native speaker's description of him or herself.
- ☐ I can *write* a one-page letter introducing myself to a foreigner.
- ☐ I can *read* a letter from a native speaker, introducing him or herself.
- ☐ I can *read* about cross-cultural relationships, and *share* my opinions.
- ☐ **Vocabulary:** I know twenty adjectives used to describe relationships.

2. Geography
- ☐ I can *read* about a famous place in the world, and answer questions.
- ☐ I can *describe* a foreign place which I have visited or read about.
- ☐ I can *answer* questions about the place that I describe.
- ☐ I can *watch* a video about a famous place, *write* questions, then *discuss* my questions.
- ☐ I can *write* about the geography of Indonesia.
- ☐ I can *answer* a foreigner's questions about the geography of Indonesia.

Vocabulary: ☐ I know thirty country names.
   ☐ I know words to describe land, water, elevation, etc.

3. Lifestyles
- ☐ I can *explain* and *answer* a foreigner's questions about life in Indonesia.
- ☐ I can *read* about life in another country, and *share* with my classmates.
- ☐ I can *listen* to a description of a different lifestyle, and *ask* questions.
- ☐ I can *compare* different lifestyles, and *talk* about positives and negatives.
- ☐ I can *write* about a desired lifestyle change for myself or someone else.
- ☐ **Vocabulary:** I know names of people and adjectives for the thirty country names that I have already learned. (Ex: Sweden, Swede, Swedish)

4. **Food**
    - ☐ I can *describe* Indonesian shopping, food preparation, and eating habits.
    - ☐ I can *write* an Indonesian recipe in English.
    - ☐ I can *understand* explanations of foreign food habits, and *ask* questions.
    - ☐ I can *compare* Indonesian food with food from other countries.
    - ☐ I can *explain* my food preferences.
    - ☐ I can *read* about nutrition around the world, and *discuss* issues.
    - ☐ I can *pray* before a meal.
    - ☐ **Vocabulary:** I know words describing food, food categories, and meals.

5. **Travel**
    - ☐ I can *describe* an Indonesian tourist attraction, and *give* advice to foreigners.
    - ☐ I can *understand* the description of an international tourist attraction.
    - ☐ I can *write* a letter giving advice to a foreigner coming to Indonesia.
    - ☐ I can *answer* the questions of a foreigner in Indonesia.
    - ☐ I can *find* tourist information on the internet; I can *understand* costs, dates, etc.
    - ☐ I can *read* tourist information in English, and *write* a letter for information.
    - ☐ I can *pray* for someone who is traveling.
    - ☐ **Vocabulary:** I know how to talk about Indonesian tourist attractions in English.

6. **Understanding Culture**
    - ☐ I can *understand* a talk about cultural differences, and *ask* questions.
    - ☐ I can *research* about a foreign culture, and *take notes*.
    - ☐ I can *give a talk* about a foreign culture, and *answer* questions.
    - ☐ I can *understand* a talk about nonverbal communication; I can *discuss* potential misunderstandings.
    - ☐ I can *role play* situations in a foreign culture, using appropriate actions and language.
    - ☐ I can *write* a paragraph on what I have learned about culture.
    - ☐ **Vocabulary:** I know at least ten words that are used in discussing culture.

7. **Holidays, Festivals, Religions**
    - ☐ I can *write* a paragraph about an Indonesian holiday, for a foreigner.
    - ☐ I can *read* about a foreign holiday, and *write* a summary.
    - ☐ I can *ask* questions of a foreigner, about special holidays.
    - ☐ I can *answer* basic questions about North American holidays.
    - ☐ I can *participate* in a holiday or tradition from another culture, knowing how to act and what to say.
    - ☐ I can *understand* a talk about major world religions, and *write* a summary.
    - ☐ **Vocabulary:** I know twenty words for holidays, festivals, and religions.
8. **Reaching Out to Others / Missions**
    - ☐ I can *read* about a world need, and *answer* questions.
    - ☐ I can *research* a world need, and *share* with my classmates.
    - ☐ I can *interview* someone about needs abroad, and *give* a report.
    - ☐ I can *read* two advertisements for charitable organizations, and *write* a comparison.
    - ☐ I can *report* on an Indonesian initiative in meeting world needs.
    - ☐ I can *discuss* Indonesia's responsibilities in the world, and *write* a letter recommending involvement.
    - ☐ **Vocabulary:** I know words to describe world needs and problems.

Christian Content
- ☐ I can *recite* Psalm 100
- ☐ I can *recite* Matthew 5:3–12 (The Beatitudes)
- ☐ I can *read* a familiar Scripture passage in an easy translation.
- ☐ I can *write* (and use) a list of worldwide prayer requests.

Ability Checklist Level 5: Personal Development

Name: _____   Dates: _____

1. **Personality / Spiritual Gifts**
    - ☐ I can *take* a personality test or spiritual gifts inventory.
    - ☐ I can *talk* about my abilities and talents in relation to jobs and activities.
    - ☐ I can *describe* my personality to a friend, and *answer* questions.
    - ☐ I can *write* a one-page summary of my personality, abilities, and talents.
    - ☐ I can *read* about someone's personality, and *ask* follow-up questions.
    - ☐ **Vocabulary:** I know thirty character-quality adjectives.

2. Life Story / Testimony
- ☐ I can *write* my personal testimony, suitable for publishing.
- ☐ I can *give* my personal testimony.
- ☐ I can *read* a short (one to two pages) biography or testimony, and *answer* questions.
- ☐ I can *ask* questions and find out about a person's past.
- ☐ I can *answer* someone's questions, telling about my past.
- ☐ **Vocabulary:** I know the words of life stages.

3. Life Adventures / Mission Trips
- ☐ I can *read* about an adventure, and *answer* questions.
- ☐ I can *interview* someone about an adventure.
- ☐ I can *write* a summary of an interview.
- ☐ I can *plan* a mission (or adventure) trip, doing research and taking notes.
- ☐ I can *present a talk* on a mission (or adventure) trip, using visuals.
- ☐ **Vocabulary:** I know nouns and adjectives for countries and people.

4. Change
- ☐ I can *read* about a changed life, and *understand* the main idea.
- ☐ I can *tell* about someone who had a significant life change.
- ☐ I can *discuss* change, and *understand* why change is difficult.
- ☐ I can *do research* about a habit that many people want to change.
- ☐ I can *give a talk* about how to achieve a desired change.
- **Vocabulary:** ☐ I know expressions for habits.
  - ☐ I can describe life change in writing and speaking.

5. Problems and Solutions
- ☐ I can *read* about a problem, and *discuss* it, giving suggestions.
- ☐ I can *write* a response to a problem, giving advice.
- ☐ I can *write* about a problem, asking for advice.
- ☐ I can *apply* biblical principles to a current problem.
- ☐ I can *pray* about a problem.
- ☐ **Vocabulary:** I know words for problems related to marriage, family, and health.

6. **Social / Christian Responsibility**
    - ☐ I can *read* about a need in another part of the world, and answer questions.
    - ☐ I can *understand* advertising (print and video) requesting charitable donations.
    - ☐ I can *do research* about a mission project or charitable organization.
    - ☐ I can *present* a report on the above, and *answer* questions.
    - ☐ I can *interview* a missionary or volunteer about his or her work.
    - ☐ I can *write* a summary of my interview for a newsletter.
    - ☐ **Vocabulary:** I know words for natural disasters and social problems.

7. **Ethical Dilemmas**
    - ☐ I can *read* about ethical issues, and *discuss* my opinion.
    - ☐ I can *participate* in a group decision on an ethical problem.
    - ☐ I can *read* about an ethical problem in our society, and *write* a response.
    - ☐ I can *write and share* a personal point of view on an ethical question.
    - ☐ **Vocabulary:** I know the words and expressions for controversial issues.

8. **Future Plans**
    - ☐ I can *understand* a talk about goal-setting.
    - ☐ I can *list* my short-term and long-term goals.
    - ☐ I can *share* my goals, and *understand* someone else's goals.
    - ☐ I can *speak clearly* about possibilities, probabilities, and certainties.
    - ☐ I can *write* a final essay about my goals and dreams, and read it to others.
    - ☐ **Vocabulary:** I know words and expressions to talk about the future.

Christian content
- ☐ I can *recite* the Ten Commandments.
- ☐ I can *recite* Psalm 1.
- ☐ I can *recite* Ephesians 6:11–13.

APPENDIX

Second Language Acquisition Self-Assessment

This is a way to assess your engagement and process in language acquisition. This assessment is meant to be used by those who are already on the field and engaged in language acquisition. It can be utilized to identify gaps in language learning and can be particularly helpful for those working with a tutor or language helper, and those who have already completed language school but find that they still have gaps in their language skills. It may also be useful for those who are just starting out. This is based on the "English for Life" task-based language learning curriculum provided in appendix B.

Name: _____

Length of time (weeks or months) in language study to date: _____

Time and Method Assessment

The chart on the following page provides an idea of the types of activities which result in language acquisition, and the relative importance of each. Read through the descriptions of each category, and note the suggested number of hours per week. Analyze your current language studies in these categories. You may likely engage in more than one of these categories in each language class. Estimate your total current time in each category, including all your current language acquisition experiences. Then, use the last column to identify any needed areas of change moving forward.

	Suggested hours/week	My current hours/week	My intended hours/week
Formal Language Acquisition: These are experiences with a teacher, tutor, or other students who are focused on opportunities to speak, listen, read, and write for meaningful communication, at your appropriate language level.	8–12		
Formal Fluency-Building: These are opportunities with a teacher, tutor, or other students to engage in repeated meaningful language use of words and structures that have already been learned, for the purpose of developing fluency.	4–5		
Formal Language Learning: These are traditional grammar, vocabulary, or pronunciation language lessons with a teacher or tutor, ideally in preparation for or to answer questions about language acquisition experiences.	4–5		
Informal Language Acquisition: These are experiences using the language outside of the classroom. Though these experiences are not controlled for language level, they must be opportunities to successfully use language that is being acquired. Simply hearing language around you, with no successful communicative engagement, does not qualify.	1–3		
Informal Language Learning: This is independent study time, such as doing homework, reading or viewing on one's own. The language studied must be at the appropriate level to qualify for this category.	3–5		
TOTAL per week	20–30		

Appendix C: Second Language Acquisition Self-Assessment

Outcomes Assessment

Go through the "English for Life" checklist (appendix B), mentally transferring it to the language you are learning. Check the items that you think you can do:

1) Without much hesitation
2) With a native speaker
3) Without too many mistakes (about 70 percent accuracy)

Do a rough calculation to come up with a percentage of your checked items. Fill in the information below according to this estimate.

Note: Following this assessment, you may want to use the "English for Life" checklist to guide your learning.

Level 1 Check

☐ I can do 80 percent or more of these tasks. My specific gaps are in these areas:
_____
_____
_____

☐ I can do about half of these tasks. I need focused lessons in these areas:
_____
_____
_____
_____

☐ I can't do very many of these tasks. I need instruction at *this* level.

Level 2 Check

☐ I can do 80 percent or more of these tasks. My specific gaps are in these areas:
_____
_____

☐ I can do about half of these tasks. I need focused lessons in these areas:
_____
_____
_____
_____

☐ I can't do very many of these tasks. I need instruction at *this* level.

Level 3 Check

☐ I can do 80 percent or more of these tasks. My specific gaps are in these areas:
_____
_____

☐ I can do about half of these tasks. I need focused lessons in these areas:
_____
_____
_____
_____

☐ I can't do very many of these tasks. I need instruction at *this* level.

Level 4 Check

☐ I can do 80 percent or more of these tasks. My specific gaps are in these areas:
_____
_____

☐ I can do about half of these tasks. I need focused lessons in these areas:
_____
_____
_____
_____

☐ I can't do very many of these tasks. I need instruction at *this* level.

Level 5 Check

☐ I can do 80 percent or more of these tasks. My specific gaps are in these areas:
_____
_____

☐ I can do about half of these tasks. I need focused lessons in these areas:
_____
_____
_____
_____

☐ I can't do very many of these tasks. I need instruction at *this* level.

APPENDIX

Language Teaching Methodologies

In 2018 I coauthored the book *Teaching English for Reconciliation: Pursuing Peace through Transformed Relationships in Language Learning and Teaching* (William Carey Publishing) with Cheryl Woelk. In that book we provide descriptions of language teaching methodologies that we have found to work well. What follows is a reprint of the "Suggested Activities" in Appendix A of that book.

Many of these are classroom language learning activities. If you are in a classroom situation, you may be able to suggest some of these activities to your teachers. Some of the activities are adaptable to tutoring situations. However you use them, I hope that reading through these activities will spark further ideas about the fun and engaging ways in which we can acquire language!

1. **Group Up**

   This whole-class activity can be used as an icebreaker or as any task to find out what the group has in common. An open-ended question (i.e., without a "right" or "wrong" answer) is called out, such as "What is your favorite color? Group up!" and students have to talk to each other in order to gather together with people who have a similar answer. After clusters have formed around the room, perhaps with a few individuals without a group, the facilitator can ask each group what their answer is. This can be a helpful activity to recognize voices on the margins that differ from the mainstream. If one person has a unique answer that doesn't fit in any group, facilitators should affirm their responses and try to find what wisdom their answer has for the group.

2. **Total Physical Response (TPR)**

   This whole-class activity can be used as an opening activity when introducing a unit or a lesson, or to provide an active break between sedentary activities. Basically, it is the process of one person making a statement that invites everyone else to respond with a physical action instead of a verbal one. In beginning language levels, it could be as simple as the teacher calling out and modeling "Stand up," "Sit down," "Turn around," and similar phrases. After modeling the first time, the teacher should refrain from performing the action, so that students can demonstrate their understanding of the language. Also, at the beginning students should not be required to speak. TPR is an excellent activity for beginning language learners precisely because it does not force students who may be in a *silent period* to speak. However, if there are students in the class who are eager to talk, students can take over the teacher's role of calling out commands, thus gaining some practice in speaking as well.

At intermediate or advanced language levels, commands or statements can be tied more specifically to content, such as "Raise your hand (or stand up) if you use Facebook" to introduce a session on cyber friendships. A follow-up could be asking students to show how often they check Facebook by holding up five fingers for several times a day to one finger for once a week or less (write this scale on the board). At high intermediate or advanced language proficiency levels, the teacher can write or speak a statement with which students could agree or disagree without judgment, such as "Students should wear uniforms in schools" to introduce a topic of schools and bullying, then ask students to line up based on how strongly they agree with the statement. Students discuss the issue with classmates in order to figure out where they stand on the topic, in relation to others' opinions. Students might then discuss why they stood where they did along the line.

3. **"I am from …"**
This writing exercise is based on George Ella Lyon's (2016) poetry writing prompt. Create a list of different categories of items related to a person's culture and identity, such as "a family tradition," "a phrase you heard often as a child," "a family food," "description of a place you went often as a child." Ask students to write their lists first. Then students add, "I am from …" before each item and add the lines together to complete the poem. This activity can be adapted to use categories appropriate for the context.

4. **Concentric Circles**
This is a whole-class activity that is a helpful way for students to practice speaking about the same topic to different partners. It requires two equally sized groups of at least three or more students. One group stands in a circle facing out. The other group stands in an outer circle facing in around the inner circle. As a result, students are paired facing another student. After engaging in discussion about the topic for a set amount of time, the outer circle moves clockwise one person and the students can discuss again with a new partner.

After the time elapses again, the inner circle moves counterclockwise and students can discuss again. This process repeats until everyone has discussed with everyone else or the total time for the activity has ended. This activity can also be done in lines rather than circles. This may spread the students out more, and make the classroom less noisy!

5. **Vocabulary Partners**

   This is an activity that is best used as a regular routine over several classes or a whole term. Students are paired with another person in class for the first session. While strategic pairing is ideal for this activity, random pairing can also work, depending on the context. Students are given time each class to work together on a vocabulary-related task, such as identifying words they are not familiar with in a reading and discerning meaning from context, or finding academic synonyms for common words in their own writing. It's usually helpful to have the same task each time the partners meet so that they can focus on completing the task rather than understanding instructions. The goal is for students to talk together to try to figure out their own understandings with the resources they have before turning to the teacher for answers. This also is a helpful way to build relationships in that a student can get to know one other student more deeply and students can support each other.

6. **Group Duties**

   This activity works well prior to any type of group task, as it entails understanding the roles that need to be fulfilled by members of the group. Depending on the students' language proficiency level, the teacher or the students prepare a list of different roles that are needed in order to complete the required task, such as "Discussion leader," "Note taker," "Turn-taking monitor," "Questioner," "Time keeper," "Summary presenter," or other roles. Then each group decides who will do each role. Optionally, the group could take turns and try out different roles for different parts of a discussion task. This activity is helpful to ensure that each group member is valued and included in the group task.

7. **Note Sorts**

   This group activity is based on a task used for group decision-making or problem-solving (Kraybill and Wright 2007). Students are given an open-ended question, such as "What ways do you enjoy learning?" or a problem to solve, such as "How can we make our school a happier place?" Then students write their answers or ideas on sticky notes, one idea or answer per note. After a set time for writing, the group silently posts their notes on the board or a spot on the wall so others in the group can also read the ideas. Students are instructed not to talk or discuss, just to read the other notes and ask only questions for clarifying understanding if needed. After everyone in the group has read the notes, they categorize them either silently, with a final discussion at the end (beginner/intermediate), or with discussion throughout (advanced). Criteria for categorization will emerge from the group and there will often, but not always, be a consensus at some point about the categorization. Finally, the group can present to the whole class the results of their ideas or answers based on categories. With more advanced language proficiency, debriefing the experience of the process can also be interesting, depending on the topic of the focus for the class.

8. **Mainstreams and Margins**

    This whole-class activity for high intermediate to advanced language proficiency learners is modified from an adult learning task designed to bring awareness of mainstream and margin dynamics in a group (Lakey 2010). In the English language class, this can be an exercise to introduce a topic that requires some empathy, related to marginalized voices. Begin with asking students to reflect silently on a time they felt left out, excluded, or on the margins. They don't need to share their story with others; just share how they felt when in that situation. Draw a large circle on the board and write the feelings that students share just outside the circle. Then ask students to reflect on characteristics of the group that would be considered "in," or "mainstream," in their situation, in essence, the characteristics of the group doing the excluding. When students share, write those characteristics on the inside of the circle. Then draw arrows from the inside of the circle to the outside and ask them to brainstorm "What could the people on the inside do to have a better relationship with the people on the outside?" Write ideas on the board. At this point, depending on the context, teachers might want to elicit how the students might understand a different perspective by reflecting on their experiences in this exercise. Alternatively, students can be asked to think about situations or times they might be more in the inside group, and share anything they might be able to do to understand the outside group in those situations. Affirm any attempts that students make at understanding another perspective.

9. **More and Less**

    This is a whole-class activity for prompting reflection on marginalization and building empathy, and is best done with older children to adult learners at any language proficiency level. The teacher prepares enough of a simple item, such as stickers, pebbles, or colored slips of paper, to distribute to five times the number in the class. Students sit in a circle and the teacher randomly hands out an uneven number of the items to each person. Some get one item, others get seven or ten, others get two, and a few get several times that of everyone else. After distributing them, ask students to reflect on how they feel. Provide feeling vocabulary (e.g., "left out," "ashamed," "ignored," "rich," "poor") according to their proficiency level ahead of time as needed. Write "more" and "less" with a line drawn between them like a continuum on the board. Ask one student to share how they feel about the number of items they received. Ask the others whether they think that student has "more" or "less," and write their feeling on the board at the appropriate place on the line. Repeat these questions until there are a number of feelings on the board between "more" and "less." Then, have the students with the most items swap with the students who had the least items and ask again how they feel and write their answers with the others. Finally, ask students to think about a time in their life when they have more or less of something and give an example, such as "more friends" or "less fun," and compare their feeling at the time to the feelings on the board. Depending on the proficiency level of the class, a follow-up could be a deeper discussion or a writing assignment.

10. **Songs**

There are many songs and worksheets for English language teaching online. On my website (https://sites.google.com/site/jandormerspage/), are a number of free, downloadable audio files of songs with accompanying worksheets, like this one:

LEAN ON ME

"… let us encourage one another …"—Hebrews 10:25

Completion

Lean on me when _____ not strong
I'll be _____ friend, I'll help you _____ on
For I know, it won't _____ long, till I'm gonna _____
Somebody to lean _____
_____ just call on me _____ when you need a _____
We all need somebody _____ lean on
I just _____ have a problem that _____ understand
We all need _____ to lean on

Idioms

Match the phrases with the definitions:

to continue	lean on
count on / rely on	call on
ask for help	carry on

Use the idioms to fill in the blanks below.

1. Can I _____ you if I need help?
2. Don't _____ on that fence. It's broken.
3. My job is difficult, but I will _____.

Questions

1. When do you "lean on" others? _____
_____
2. Can others "lean on" you? How and when? _____
_____

11. Dicto-Comp

This combination of dictation and composition (adapted from Wajnryb 1988) can be used successfully for older children and adults. It practices all four skills (reading, writing, speaking, and listening), and helps students develop accuracy in language use. Begin with a short (3–4 sentences) paragraph that is written at the students' language level and that is meaningful to them. The advantage for peace-building goals is that you can choose a paragraph which helps further those goals. For example, I chose the paragraph below to help intermediate-level learners consider the potential in the simple action of smiling. Where English is concerned, the paragraph also models the use of helping verbs, such as can, could, should, might, etc.

> Have you ever thought about the value of a smile? A smile can make those around you feel better. A smile could help to resolve a conflict, even more than the words you say. And smiling at your teacher might even help you get better grades! Of course, a smile should be genuine. But even if you don't feel like smiling, smiling can make you feel better.

After selecting a paragraph, follow these steps:

1. Introduce the topic so that students will be prepared for the text.
   This could include asking questions, showing pictures, or introducing vocabulary words.
2. Read the paragraph to the students. Do not allow them to write anything down.
3. Read the paragraph again, allowing students to take notes. Repeat this step a few times, if necessary.
4. Ask students to rewrite the paragraph, based on their notes. Give them these guidelines:
   - Their writing should have the same ideas.
   - Their writing should be grammatically correct.
   - Their writing does not need to be exactly like the paragraph you read.

5. In groups of 3–4, have students share their paragraphs, and come up with a group version.
6. Students write their group versions on the board or on large papers which can be put on the wall.
7. The teacher reads each paragraph as it is completed, underlining parts that may need work. Groups gather around their versions, correcting them and soliciting the teacher's help as needed.
8. All groups read their paragraphs to the class.

12. Surveys

Surveys are an excellent activity in language classrooms, as they provide the opportunity to ask the same question again and again, to different classmates. The teacher provides a table which students fill out as they go around the room asking their classmates the specified questions. The question and answer prompts are provided on the survey sheet, so that students will practice the desired language forms. Surveys are very helpful in language development, especially for beginners. Surveys can also be instrumental in achieving reconciliatory teaching goals, as they can be very relational. Surveys can have students asking each other questions about likes, dislikes, experiences, beliefs, opinions, and more. In this way, they are a great tool to help classmates get to know one another better. Here is an example:

Q: Do you like _____?

A: 👍 Yes, I like _____.

👎 No, I don't like _____.

Name	bananas	apples	papaya	pineapple
Mario	√	√	X	√

13. Interviews

In surveys, students ask the same question to many people. In interviews, they ask different questions to the same person. Thus, interviews can help students develop and use more language, and they can also build relationships at a deeper level. Interviews can be used at all language levels beyond very beginning. The lower the language level, the more important it is to *guide* the interview task. A guided interview assignment is shown below.

In this task the teacher first directs students to write their interview questions on the chart. After students have attempted this, the teacher might engage in whole-class instruction to check the questions. Then, students will be paired for the interview, and students will write their partner's answers on their chart. Finally, students will use the guided writing model to write a short paragraph about their partner.

Write about Your Friend!

Ask your friend:	Question	Answer
Name		
Country		
Age		
Birthday		
Sisters		
Brothers		
Hobbies		

My friend is _____. _____ comes from _____. _____ is _____ years old. _____ birthday is on _____. _____ has _____ sisters and _____ brothers. _____ likes to _____. I like my new _____!

This kind of interview template and process can be changed in many ways, for different language levels and for different purposes. For example, the interviews could focus on where students have lived, or cultural differences, or opinions about something the teacher has had students read or view. The possibilities are endless!

14. **Find Someone Who …**

This familiar icebreaker game also has a lot of potential in the English language classroom. Teachers can create lists that will help to both build relationships and practice English, based on their knowledge of the students in the classroom. Students go around asking their classmates if they can answer "yes" to any of the questions, and collecting signatures. This activity can work well at any level, as long as the language used is at the students' level. The sample below might work well for low intermediate levels and above. In this sample, students gain practice paying attention to the presence or absence of "s" on the verb (e.g., "Find someone who writes …" changed to "Do you write … ?"). This activity is also excellent for relationship-building, as it gets students thinking about the issue of stress and coping mechanisms. When students talk with a partner after the "find someone who" activity, they may be able to share at a deeper level about the stressors they experience.

How do your classmates cope with stress? Find someone who …
1. writes in a journal   Name: _____
   Question prompt: **Do you write … ?**
2. talks to a friend   Name: _____
3. talks to a family member   Name: _____
4. eats ice cream   Name: _____
5. goes shopping   Name: _____
6. goes running   Name: _____
7. reads a book   Name: _____
8. other: _____   Name: _____

Write then talk with a partner:
Do any of your classmates cope with stress in the same way that you do?
_____
Would you like to change how you cope with stress?
_____
Does your partner have any advice for coping with stress?
_____

For lower level classes, students could be asked to find classmates who like different colors, have certain numbers of siblings, have had certain kinds of health issues, go to specific places, like different sports … and much more!

15. Upset the Fruit Basket
This is a well-known circle game that can be adapted for language practice. It is yet another activity which not only helps students practice certain vocabulary or language structures, but which can also help them to get to know each other. The game is played with everyone sitting in a circle (divide into two circles if the class is large), with one person standing in the middle. That person says something which causes others to move. When they move, the person in the middle tries to get one of the seats.

In a beginning class where students have been learning about families, the teacher might provide the prompt, "Move if you …" along with some possible sentence endings: "Move if you have a brother," or "Move if you have two grandparents." In a more advanced class, the teacher might set up a prompt like this one, focusing on present perfect:

"I haven't ever _____. Move if you *have*. GO!"
And then switch it to:
"I have _____. Move if you *haven't*. GO!"

It is helpful to present the prompts and have students write down some possibilities before you begin playing the game, as it is difficult to "think on your feet" in a second language. It is also helpful to teach students to wait for the word GO before they move. This allows language learners more time to process the statement and decide whether they need to move or not.

16. Circle Practice

Students and teacher sit in a circle. The teacher begins by speaking a word, phrase, or question to a student next to her. That student repeats it to the next student, and so on. Often an exchange can be practiced, such as the following:

T: This is an apple (handing the student an apple).
S1: What?
T: An apple.
S1: This is an apple.
S2: What?
S1: An apple.
S2: This is an apple.

And the apple continues around the circle. If this activity is being used for *review* rather than for introducing new content, the teacher may start a second phrase after the first has been done by one or two students. For more fun (and confusion!) start another phrase going in the opposite direction around the circle!

References

Kraybill, R., and E. Wright. 2007. *The Little Book of Cool Tools for Hot Topics: Group Tools to Facilitate Meetings When Things Are Hot*. Good Books. Retrieved from https://books.google.ca/books?id=hiNrAAAACAAJ.

Lakey, G. 2010. *Facilitating Group Learning: Strategies for Success with Adult Learners*. John Wiley & Sons. Retrieved from https://books.google.ca/books?id=U9iZT58ls8MC.

Lyon, G. E. 2016. "Where I'm From." Retrieved from http://www.georgeellalyon.com/where.html.

Wajnryb, R. 1988. "The Dictogloss Method of Language Teaching: A Text-based, Communicative Approach to Grammar." *English Teaching Forum* 26, no. 3:35–38.

APPENDIX

Language Learning Resources to Create

Many of these resources can involve the whole family!

1. **Labels.** One of the first and simplest things you can do to assist your language learning is to label items around your house. Don't create dozens of labels at the very beginning—that can be overwhelming! Instead, as you learn each new category of words, label those things in your house. For example, when you learn furniture, label all the furniture in your house. When you learn clothing, hang various articles of clothing in a prominent place, with labels on them. Likewise, you can label food, people in photos, and colors in a painting. You can make a fun family game out of "labeling" each other to learn body parts! You can even take photos of various activities, and create verb labels to go with them. To avoid clutter and to test your memory, remove words that you think you have learned, just reinstating those that you have difficulty remembering.
2. **Matching cards.** Sets of matching words and pictures can be used for many fun activities. If possible, take photos of local items, rather than just finding random pictures online. Here are some activities that you can do with matched sets of words and pictures:
   - **Memory game:** Lay all cards face down. Take turns turning over two. If the two are a word-picture match, the player keeps the pair and goes again. If not, the two cards are turned back face down, and stay in place. Play continues until all pairs have been matched. The person with the most pairs wins.
   - **Go fish:** Each player takes five cards. During a turn, a player asks one other player for a card that matches a word or picture in her hand. If the player asked does not have the card, she says "Go fish," indicating that the player should pick up a card from the deck.
   - **Speed match:** Time yourself matching all the words and pictures. Then mix up cards and try to beat your time.

3. **Songs and chants.** It's not too difficult to put new words to familiar tunes, and sing your way to remembering new phrases and words. Chants are similarly effective, as the rhythms stick in your brain, helping you to remember. Some languages lend themselves more to rhythm than others, so check with a language helper to make sure your songs and chants are helping you, for example to learn correct rhythm and intonation.
4. **Board games.** All you need are a die and markers and a piece of paper to use the familiarity of a board game to practice language. Draw a free-form "board," and mark off squares. Write some kind of prompt for language production in each of the squares. When someone rolls the die and lands on that square, they must produce that language. Here are some examples of prompts and tasks:
   - Times (4:30 a.m.; 8:00 p.m., etc.). Make a complete sentence about what you do at that time of day.
   - Food items. State whether you like that item. Or to make it more complex, how you might prepare it.
   - Activities. State the last time or the next time you will do that activity.
   - Prepositions. Make a sentence with that preposition.
   - Verb tenses. Make a sentence using that verb tense.
   - Colors. Make a sentence telling about something related to that color.
5. **Tic-tac-toe.** Create a 3 by 3 square grid, and write new words in the squares. You can only "X" or "O" that square after you have made a sentence using that word. For a simpler version, create X's and O's out of paper clips, twist-ties, or paper. Place cards with pictures or words in the form of a tic-tac-toe grid. As you make your sentences using the words, place your X or O on top of the word or picture.
6. **Posters.** If you have an artistic bent, you might enjoy creating inspirational, humorous, or aesthetically pleasing posters utilizing your new language. For example, they might contain Scripture verses or list common polite phrases. Turing the new language into something you would enjoy decorating your walls with can be very motivating!
7. **Audio recordings.** Sometimes recordings that you produce by yourself, or with other students, can provide better listening material than something commercially produced or created by native speakers of the language. The latter might go too fast and use many words you don't know. Producing your own recordings can give you an opportunity to hear the same language repeatedly, committing it to memory. Here are some examples:
   - Interviews. Interview your teacher or another student—or be interviewed by them.

- "How to" session. Record yourself telling how to do something—maybe even make it a video! Examples could include following a recipe, doing a craft, selecting the best fruit at the market, cleaning something, etc.

8. **Sentence frames and sentence starters.** A sentence frame is a sentence with blanks in it, where key words would be inserted. A sentence starter provides the beginning of the sentence, and you fill in the rest. These exercises are staples in language classrooms, either written on the board or on posters around the room. You can create your own sentences to help you practice using the language at home. Here are some examples:
   - I am wearing _____, _____, and _____. (Fill in with your articles of clothing, or the colors you are wearing.)
   - Yesterday I _____, then I _____. (Fill in with two things you did yesterday.)
   - I am too _____ to _____. (Fill in with an adjective and activity.)
   - Can I buy some … (Fill in all the things you need to buy.)
   - I feel … (Describe your feeling.)
   - Yesterday I felt … (Describe your feeling yesterday.)
   - I am happy/sad/discouraged/encouraged because …

9. **A Picture Dictionary.** Picture dictionaries can be purchased in many languages (check out http://www.esl.net/oxford_picture_dictionary.html#:~:text=). However, creating your own will help you learn more language and will also include pictures connected to your own context. Here are some suggestions that may help you:
   - Take photos of real items representing the words that you want to learn. In the beginning these might mostly be nouns. But you can easily expand to photos illustrating verbs, adjectives, and adverbs.
   - You might want to upload your photos into Word documents, print them off, and create real books. Or you might want to create your "book" on your phone or computer.
   - Consider creating two versions for each word set: one with the written word and one without. This will allow you to practice remembering the word, as you begin to learn it just by looking at the picture.
   - Usually it's not advisable to include the English definition. The point is to link the word in your new language directly to the picture.

10. **Proficiency Goals.** Personalize your learning by creating your own specific language-learning goals. You can use any of the proficiency scale descriptions in appendix A or the *English for Life* system in appendix B as a starting point. The value of creating your own proficiency goals or "can do" statements is to set very specific learning goals for yourself, contextualized to your own needs and setting. Here are some examples:
    - I can accurately say amounts of money when paying for something in the market or receiving change.

- I can ask about my helper's children when I greet her in the morning, and understand her responses.
- I have memorized the words to five simple choruses, I am able to sing them during my own personal or our family devotional time, and I can understand what I am singing.

Make sure that your personalized goals are motivating and achievable. Add realistic time frames if it would provide additional motivation for you. For example, when you are beginning to learn numbers and how to say amounts of money, you might determine that within two weeks you will use those number words when you purchase items in the market. And as you begin to hear songs in the local language at church, you might decide that within two months you would like to have memorized five of them. Personalized goals can be helpful if they are both motivating and do-able.

APPENDIX

Language Learning Online Resources

New online resources for language learning are being developed all the time. Increasingly, applications for computers and phones can provide helpful resources for your language acquisition. Here are a few websites that I have found helpful:

Free Language Learning Apps
   https://www.pcmag.com/authors/jill-duffy

Free Language Learning Websites
   https://www.fluentu.com/blog/free-language-learning-websites/
   http://www.bbc.co.uk/languages/

Free Online Language Level Tests
   https://www.cactuslanguage.com/language-level-tests/
   https://www.languagelevel.com/

Proficiency Resources

ACTFL (AMERICAN COUNCIL OF TEACHERS OF FOREIGN LANGUAGES)
   https://www.actfl.org/publications/guidelines-and-manuals/actfl-proficiency-guidelines-2012

COMMON EUROPEAN FRAMEWORK OF REFERENCE (CEFR)
   https://www.youtube.com/watch?v=UAehOcVfr3Y
   https://tracktest.eu/english-levels-cefr/

Pronunciation Websites
   https://forvo.com/
   https://cegepenglish.zendesk.com/hc/en-us/articles/201230465-A-List-of-Websites-that-Will-Pronounce-Specific-Words-or-Sounds-for-You

ACKNOWLEDGMENTS

This book is the product of experiences and learning that could not have been possible without the input, guidance, and help of many people along the way. First, my TESOL colleagues, especially those who also understand the mission community, have provided invaluable insights. Many read chapters and provided feedback. Others have spoken into my life and professional growth over the years, helping me to become the TESOL professional that I am today. I am deeply grateful for these colleagues, and I endeavor to invest in others the way they have invested in me.

Second, perhaps my best teachers over the years have been my students. To my former English-learning students in Canada, Indonesia, Brazil, Kenya, and other places... thank you for allowing me to be a part of your language acquisition, and to learn along the way how classroom activities can translate into language competence. I greatly appreciate those of you who remain close friends and colleagues many years later. You are a treasured part of my life.

I would also like to thank two students at Messiah University who helped analyze the data from the missionary language learning survey. Emily Stark and Mauree Shott, your work lives on through this book!

Third, I am grateful for my colleagues in missions. Like many MKs, I grew up viewing my missionary family as my aunts and uncles and cousins. As an adult missionary, I came to understand the complex issues in missions, especially given changes in the world and in cross-cultural ministry. However, my affection and appreciation for the larger missionary family has not diminished. Though I now work in higher education, I still feel most like an "insider" in mission circles, and appreciate the experiences, both good and difficult, on various "mission fields" which have served as a foundation for this book.

Finally, I am indebted to my family. My parents, Max and Dixie Edwards, obeyed God's calling, leaving a thriving farm life in rural Indiana to minister in Brazil. A small part of their story—and my childhood story—is told in this book. (Their full story is told in the book *Boldly I Obey*, published by One Mission Society.) I am grateful for my parents' openness to have their story told.

You will also read quite a bit about my immediate family in these pages. My daughters, Danna Jo and Jenna, went through more changes than most in their growing-up years. They were born in Canada, started school in Indonesia, moved to Brazil for five years, then finished high school back in Indonesia. The fact that they are well adjusted in life now, having added to our family two very special sons-in-law and three adorable grandsons, is a testimony to God's grace and their own strong faith throughout the upheavals during their growing up years. I thank them for letting me freely tell their stories!

My life partner and best friend, Rod, has struggled to learn both Indonesian and Portuguese during our years on the field. Though living with a professional language educator should have made this easier, I'm quite certain that at times it didn't! The difficulties he has faced in language learning have helped me see language learner struggles in a new way. But even more than that, his persistence in language learning let

Acknowledgments

me see the heart of a man passionate for discipleship and the equipping of pastors to reach their own. I have had a front-row seat to the ministry of two individuals, my dad and my husband, who would not be qualified for overseas ministry if the measure were language aptitude. I got to see two men who love the Lord with all their hearts have a long-lasting impact in their countries of service, despite, and sometimes because of, their difficulties with the language. This, probably more than anything else, drove the writing of this book.

I thank God for the experiences, education, support from others, time, energy, and insights to write this book. It all comes from him. May he use these pages to help you in some small way along the path to and in your calling.

CPSIA information can be obtained
at www.ICGtesting.com
Printed in the USA
LVHW050131070121
675887LV00019B/2748